The Geriatric Pilgrim

Tales from the Journey

by Richard Wile

The Geriatric Pilgrim: Tales from the Journey
Copyright © 2023 Richard Wile

ISBN: 978-1-63381-332-8

All rights reserved. No part of this book may be reproduced in any form or by any electronic or mechanical means, including information storage and retrieval systems, without permission in writing from the author, except by a reviewer, who may quote brief passages in review.

Image "Albert György, Mélancolie, 2012" was posted to Flickr by art_inthecity at https://flickr.com/photos/57286185@N04/44551153491
License: https://creativecommons.org/licenses/by/4.0/

Designed and produced by:
Maine Authors Publishing
12 High Street, Thomaston, Maine
www.maineauthorspublishing.com

Printed in the United States of America

*For Mary Lee, who asked,
"Do you dance slow?"*

Table of Tales

Welcome 1

No Matter How Much You Prepare, You'll Never Be Ready. 3
Betwixt and Between 7
Pilgrimage as Exile 11
Joy and the Banjo 15
Gifts 20
The Path Is Made by Walking 24
A Pilgrim's Journal: April 22, 1999 28
Waldo and Henry 32
Healed Doesn't Mean Cured 36
Edu-cations 39
The Dark Woods 43
Some Stones from the Journey 46
Baseball as Pilgrimage 51
The Fugitive in the Photo 54
A Pilgrim's Journal: August 9, 2002 59
Being in Tanzania 62
Food for the Journey 66
Back Story 69
The Stories We Carry 74
Our Embedded Remains 78
We Pilgrims 81
A Pilgrim's Journal: August 9, 2003 85

Stan	88
The Annual Pilgrimage	92
Work as Pilgrimage	96
On Emptiness	101
Rooting Around	104
Thin Places	108
A Pilgrim's Journal: September 23, 2010	112
The River	116
Scars	119
Pilgrimage to City Lights	122
On Hope	126
Names I've Carried	130
Here Comes the Judge!	134
The Pattern of Exodus	138
A Pilgrim's Journal: March 19, 2011	142
Sunday Afternoon Drives	146
Pilgrimage to Riverside	150
Have Snakeskin, Will Travel	153
The Climbing Tree	157
A Pilgrim's Journal: August 2019	160
Confessions of an Introvert	166
Up to the Garden	170
Showing Up	174
Putting Away the Past	178
Navigating the Death of an Ex	181
A Pilgrim's Journal: July 2021	185
Dancing Lessons	189
Where I Need to Be	192
With Gratitude	196

The Geriatric Pilgrim

Welcome

Ten years ago, my wife, Mary Lee, and I made a walking pilgrimage along St. Cuthbert's Way, from Melrose, Scotland, to the Holy Island of Lindisfarne, off the east coast of England. Although we'd taken several trips before then that I would now call pilgrimages, it wasn't until walking St. Cuthbert's Way and reading books about the pilgrim experience that I realized not only had those earlier trips been pilgrimages, but that I could look at my entire life as a pilgrimage.

What do I mean by that word? Well, I'd say a pilgrimage is a journey—both external and internal—made to a place of personal significance; a passage across a threshold between the old and the new; an exploration to discover new dimensions of ourselves; an adventure where we relinquish or surrender or have taken from us certainty and control; an odyssey in which we return home with renewed awareness, seeing the familiar in new ways.

Viewing my life as a pilgrimage, I've found, has helped me—at the age of eighty—to become more curious, to look for surprises, to live without planning every detail, to put myself in uncomfortable situations—even if it's just going for a walk and having no destination or facilitating a creative writing class at a drop-in center for the homeless. I'm learning to embrace the unknown, including a higher power totally outside my understanding, and to look for evidence of that higher power—what I would call grace—all around me.

About six years ago, I began writing a blog called "The Geriatric Pilgrim," detailing my various journeys. Now, I've revised some of those reflections for this book. In the process—which has become another kind of pilgrimage—I've been amazed by how both I and the world have changed over the last six years. What hasn't changed is that whether I'm writing about palpable pilgrimages to sites in the United States, Great Britain, Israel, Turkey, Tanzania, or the pond behind my house, my real journey has been to find healing from growing up in an alcoholic family, from the death of my eighteen-year-old daughter, and these days, from growing old during a worldwide pandemic.

So, unlike other books I've read on pilgrimage, I'm not writing about the eccentric personalities Mary Lee and I met on our travels, or of coming home cured of COPD. Rather, I'm reflecting on my various journeys through grief and grace with the mystery I've come to call God of My Not Understanding.

I'm hoping these musings will remind you of the pilgrimages you've made and the lessons you've learned along your way.

No Matter How Much You Prepare, You'll Never Be Ready.

MARY LEE AND I FIRST STARTED TALKING ABOUT GOING ON A walking pilgrimage after seeing the film *The Way*, in which Martin Sheen's character walks the El Camino de Santiago from the Pyrenees through the interior of northern Spain to Santiago de Compostela to honor his son who'd died making that pilgrimage. Reading about the five hundred miles of the Camino, however, convinced us that it was nothing two people dancing around seventy were ready for, so we began looking at other pilgrimages, eventually finding St. Cuthbert's Way, a sixty-two-mile hike from Melrose on the Scottish border, where one of the early English church's most revered saints started his religious life in AD 650, to the Holy Island of Lindisfarne off the Northumberland coast, where he served as both prior and bishop.

    For the next six months, we prepared. We booked our flights to and from Edinburgh. We researched travel companies who reserve B&Bs, transport luggage, provide information about where to stay and what to see and where to eat each day. We watched every YouTube video there was on St. Cuthbert's Way. I read ten books on pilgrimages, hiking trips, and St. Cuthbert. (Bibliography available upon request.) We increased our walking from one to four miles a day, with longer walks on the weekends. Because the last two miles of St. Cuthbert's Way are traditionally walked barefoot at low tide across to Holy Island, we walked

Maine's beaches carrying our shoes around our necks like amulets against injuries that I was afraid might keep us from going. (And against which I took out travel insurance, just in case.)

All this led to multiple trips to L.L. Bean for walking sticks, backpacks, water bladders, a compass, a pedometer, two hiking skirts for Mary Lee, a fleece jacket for me, microfiber underwear and a half dozen pairs of socks for each of us. I went to a podiatrist, who looked at my high arches and prescribed custom orthotics. I had my annual physical, my annual eye exam, and my semiannual dentist visit to make sure I was prepared.

Intellectually prepared, yes. Emotionally ready, no.

Our first surprise came the night before we started hiking. Nothing I read had told us that when Melrose Abbey closes, nobody checks to see if there's anyone still on the grounds before locking the gates. So that to leave, Mary Lee and I had to clamber up a stone wall and hoist ourselves over a wrought-iron fence designed by Vlad the Impaler.

And do you think we could find the beginning of St. Cuthbert's Way? Not until we'd walked by it three times. No one tells you that the start of the way, marked on a sign with words about the size of the bottom row of print on my eye exam chart, is through an alley, past two trash bins, and down a cement walk. It's only after you make a left and walk a muddy path around a hill that you find the 133 wooden steps that mark the real beginning of the pilgrimage.

And if 133 steps sounds like a lot, they were only the beginning of our climb up the Eildon Hills. Nothing I read, nothing I saw prepared me for the up-and-down nature of St. Cuthbert's Way. To be honest, there's nothing really high (Wideopen Hill, at 1208 feet, is the highest point) or sheer or steep, unless you're from Southern Maine, where we call a 485-foot pimple on the face of the landscape Bradbury Mountain. I would estimate that we spent about two-thirds of our walk either going up or coming down. Our legs were fine; our wind was not.

The guidebooks, the videos don't talk about shit. Many show bucolic photographs of sheep and cows dotting the countryside, but none show them standing and defecating on your path. Once we had to walk through a dozen young bulls, and while they all moved out of our way, what they deposited didn't.

On the other hand, nothing I saw or read prepared me for the beauty of gorse bushes in the fog, their spiky branches laced with dew-covered spider webs, the huge oaks and sycamores and maples and beeches whose gnarled roots and branches look like something out of J.R.R. Tolkien, a flock of white geese splashing in the River Teviot, the ruins of three lovely abbeys and a castle, the smell of wild garlic, the sight of feral goats, the views from Wideopen Hill and the Cheviots, acres of purple heather, the cool eeriness of St. Cuthbert's Cave, our first glimpse of the ocean, the wild sound of seals as we walked across the sands to Lindisfarne.

* * *

This pilgrimage reminds me of other times when I've been prepared but not ready. I had plenty of time, for example, to prepare for the death of my eighteen-year-old daughter. Three months after Laurie was diagnosed in March with primitive neuroectodermal tumor (PNET), the doctors at Dana Farber were clear that her chances of survival were slim. When, after radiation and chemotherapy, cancer reappeared in her pelvis in September, those chances dropped to nothing. Her mother and I spent the next three months preparing for her death. The day after Laurie died, two days before Christmas, I recall telling one of the nurses I'd already done my grieving and was now going to start living again.

Talk about bullshit. Nothing I had done, felt, or imagined made me ready for the next (as I write) thirty-four years: the anger, the guilt, the tears, the terror, the demolition of all I'd ever believed about life, the universe, and everything. Nor, on the other hand, did I ever expect ever-increasing moments of joy and gratitude.

Even after all these years, I can feel my body chemistry change around Halloween. And I can prepare for that. What I am never ready for is how I will react each year. Some years, I tried to sleep for two months; some years, I wrote suicidal short stories; some years, angry letters to the editor or to people who pissed me off. One year, after my cranky back being almost pain-free for a year or more, it throbbed and burned until December 24th, the day after the anniversary of Laurie's death. After Christmas, the pain was gone.

At the same time, nothing in those months by Laurie's side in the hospital prepared me for the way she entered first, my dreams, then, my waking life. Her voice in my ear ("Look at that, Dad!") as the sun rose over the island of Lindisfarne. Her hand on my shoulder as Mary Lee and I sat on the side of Wideopen Hill eating our cheese and pickle sandwiches. The joy that I continue to get from her ongoing presence. Since Laurie died, I have never felt so godforsaken and broken. I have also never felt so fortunate and grateful.

These days, thanks to my epidemiologist daughter-in-law, Mary Lee and I have been as prepared as anyone for the next phase of the coronavirus. Daniele convinced us to cancel a retreat to Arizona when the pandemic first hit this country, and the next year advised us that, if we wanted to take a European river cruise, we should do it immediately because the virus was between waves. But we were not ready—and still aren't—for either the frustrations of outdoor church services and anxieties for our school-age grandchildren during this pandemic, or the joys of slowing down to appreciate the lady's slippers in the woods or a good mystery by the fireplace.

Of course, it's important to prepare—who am I to argue with the Boy Scouts?—but as walking St. Cuthbert's Way reminded me, the best way to prepare for any pilgrimage is to get ready for surprises.

Betwixt and Between

THE WORD *LIMINALITY*, FROM THE LATIN, LIMENS, MEANS "STANDING at the threshold." Basically, it means betwixt and between—professionally, socially, spiritually, whatever. You've moved out of one house but haven't yet moved into a new one, or you've left one stage in your life and haven't yet entered the next one.

As I write, the world has been living in liminality since late December 2019, when people in Wuhan, China, began to get sick from a previously unknown pneumonia. COVID-19 ended the life I had been leading for almost eighty years—a world of handshakes and hugs and plenty of toilet paper, a world without masks, without Pfizer and Moderna. And as to what happens next, well God only knows. If I'm still alive, I may find that the world has learned to live together more compassionately, or that democracy as I've known it has gone the way of the twenty-three species (eleven birds, eight freshwater mussels, two fish, one bat, and one plant) officially declared extinct in 2021.

What gives me hope is to look back at the travels and pilgrimages I've made as kinds of liminality. When I'm on pilgrimage, I'm on a threshold between cultures, sometimes between identities. I've left the United States and have not yet arrived in Scotland or Israel or Turkey. I've walked off the English mainland but haven't yet set foot on the island of Lindisfarne. I'm suspended between worlds, a stranger (which is what the word *peregrini*—the root of pilgrim—means) to both the past and the future.

There are places that are in and of themselves liminal, actual spaces where I've literally been betwixt and between: airports, bus terminals, and train stations; hotels and motels; retreat houses; hospitals. Each has a unique energy that rubs off on me. Airports and their like I find exotic—people dressed in various costumes scurrying like mad under weird lighting or zonked-out in dark corners. I become a character in a suspense novel, about to board the Orient Express. Retreat houses, especially those connected with monasteries are, of course, silent and contemplative, and I automatically lower my voice and move more slowly, become more aware. Hospitals are for me a surrealistic mosaic of pain and relief, selfishness and kindness, sorrow and happiness, where I'm conscious of my ignorance, my fragility, my mortality.

When I think of other liminal times in my life, I also recall having had mixed experiences. Twenty-five years ago, I had bilateral hip surgery and was laid up for eight weeks. The throbbing hip pain I'd suffered for ten years was gone, but I hadn't yet learned how to walk again. Moreover, as I spent my days reading and watching exercise programs on TV, I realized how much I was enjoying not being in a classroom and that it was time to close the door on a thirty-year public school teaching career, even though I had no idea what door was going to open afterward. I recall being apprehensive (okay, I was scared stiff), not only about how Mary Lee and I could survive economically, but about who I would be if I weren't *Mr. Wile*, my identity for thirty years. But at the same time, a feeling of absolute determination took hold. By the end of those eight weeks, I knew, knew as thoroughly as I knew the date of my birth, that I could no longer remain a high school English teacher.

Thinking of places that have been both physically and emotionally liminal, I recall that when I was between marriages, I lived for six months in a one-room apartment. This was a convoluted time of tearing down one relationship (with my ex-wife), remodeling another relationship (with my daughter), and building a completely new relationship (with the woman I planned to marry). I was sad, angry, frustrated, hopeful, joyous—sometimes within two hours and three phone calls. I don't believe I've ever felt so alive in my life.

On the other hand, one of the most painful periods of my life was the two months I lived in a Ronald McDonald House 120 miles from home. My daughter's cancer had confined her to a hospital room. I'd taken a leave of absence from teaching and left Mary Lee and her son behind in order to be by her side. It was clear by then that Laurie's condition was terminal, but she hadn't died. My image of God had died, and I hadn't yet come up with a new one. Every day, when I wasn't at the hospital, I went back to the Ronald McDonald House and ate and slept and occasionally talked with fellow pilgrims on this journey none of us wanted to be on, wishing the whole damn thing would just be over.

But although I didn't know it at the time, I can see now that a big part of who I am today was forged during those two months. Laurie and I shared with each other in ways we'd never been able to do. In the hospital cafeteria, at the Ronald McDonald House, by my daughter's bed while she slept, I read Thomas Merton, Henri Nouwen, Camus, the Bible, and the mystics. I wrote continually in journals, in the margins of the books I was reading, sometimes on cafeteria napkins. I've been rebuilding my life from that foundation ever since.

Pilgrimages and retreats grow out of spiritual traditions which recognize that although liminality can be painful, it's essential for growth. According to Richard Rohr, one of my spiritual gurus, liminal spaces are realms of "pure possibility...when...we can begin to think and act in genuinely new ways." The temporary liminality of pilgrimages and retreats helps prepare us for these betwixt-and-between times in our lives, those times when one door has closed and another door hasn't yet opened. They offer practice in being receptive and living in the moment.

I need this practice. More and more these days, I can feel other doors, in addition to those slammed shut by this pandemic, closing behind me. Almost every week, it seems, I find something else I used to be able to do but no longer can: put a basketball through a hoop, touch the ceiling or the floor, open jars, stay awake after ten o'clock, remember where I put my car keys. The doors ahead of me that I can see—retirement communities, assisted living, nursing homes, and of course the Great Door of Death—haven't yet opened.

I'm not comfortable with this space in between. I want to fill it with memories of the past, often a past that never was: I was stronger, the food tasted better, life was simpler, I was happier; or plan for a future I will later find doesn't exist, at least not in the way I imagined it, especially since I tend to "awfulize," as we say in Al Anon, creating scary scenarios about cancerous tumors or debilitating strokes or dementia, an even more serious strain of virus, of slowly starving because of not having enough money to go into a decent nursing home.

I need to focus on today, on what I can do now that I never did before—watch birds and grandchildren, take on new writing projects, read more on how different spiritual traditions can help me understand my own experiences, work to bring sanity to our government, lend a hand to others.

And, even though COVID and age may cut down my traveling, I need to keep seeing myself as pilgrim, as a "stranger," betwixt and between, standing on that threshold, open to possibility.

Pilgrimage as Exile

I PROBABLY BEGAN THINKING ABOUT THE WORD *PILGRIMAGE* JUST before the trip Mary Lee and I took to Jerusalem in the summer of 1997. Before we left, I read a magazine article in which the author distinguished between pilgrims and tourists. Tourists, she wrote, go out from the center of their worlds, their homes, to vacation; pilgrims, on the other hand, seek to travel from the edges of their lives to their center, their homes. Well, that sounded like a pretty good distinction to me. Good churchgoers that we are, Mary Lee and I were, I thought, going "home" to the origin of our faith.

However, while Mary Lee had a great time, my trip felt like being exiled to the fiery furnace of Hell. Every day the temperature soared to well over ninety degrees. Within two days I had picked up an intestinal bug and was popping Lomotil like sunflower seeds. From the moment we arrived, we were lost. The first day we wandered for three hours through the labyrinth of streets and alleyways of the Old City of Jerusalem looking for the street back to St. George's Cathedral Guest House and its friendly hollyhocks and British accents. The next day we found ourselves locked in the Garden of Gethsemane outside the Old City and wandering blindly on the backside of the Mount of Olives.

On Friday, back in the Old City, we joined the Franciscan Friars on their Walk of Devotion up the Via Dolorosa to the Church of the Holy

Sepulchre, built where tradition says Jesus was crucified and buried. Walk of Agony was more like it. If you've never been to the Old City of Jerusalem, know that those damned cobblestone streets rise at least forty-five degrees. Every twenty steps, my ailing gut felt as if one of the ubiquitous Israeli soldiers had kicked it with a combat boot. Swarms of young boys tried to pull us into booths featuring five-foot posters of baby Jesus and the Virgin, baskets of wooden rosaries, and passages of scripture woven on dishtowels.

The Church of the Holy Sepulchre was a sauna. Mary Lee and I were funneled up a set of stairs into a second-floor room where Jesus hung on a cross, wearing what looked like a silver diaper, his head covered from ear to ear with a semicircle of tin. Cameras flashed. Voices babbled. Smells of incense, body odor, and stale cigarettes assailed us.

On the first floor, the Holy Sepulchre itself looked like a block of dirty cement. A man with a long black beard and a tall black hat berated a woman for having bare shoulders. More cramps as people pushed me through a doorway into damp sour air, candles, aluminum icons, and Jesus wearing another tin hat.

The place felt about as holy as a sardine factory.

* * *

The next day, I sat on a bench in the Garden Tomb, just outside the Old City walls, the alternative site of Jesus's burial. In 1882, General Charles Gordon, Bible student and British soldier, decided this site and not the Church of the Holy Sepulchre was where Jesus had been taken after his death. Yellow and red roses covered the stones, and cool, shaded paths wound under cypress, palm, and pine trees to a large platform with wooden benches looking out over "Skull Hill," where Gordon thought the crucifixion had happened. Below me was the cave where Jesus had supposedly been interred. Earlier, when Mary Lee and I had gone inside, the rock upon which the body would have been laid was smooth and looked as if you could lie down on it and get a good night's sleep.

Pilgrimage as Exile

I inhaled the fragrance of the flowers and the trees, watched swallows swoop through the leaves, and felt more at peace than I had in all the sweat, discomfort, and confusion of the last few days.

This was when I knew that I was in the wrong place for Jesus's crucifixion and burial.

I remembered nine years earlier, when each day for two months I walked from the Ronald McDonald House to the Eastern Maine Medical Center, where my eighteen-year-old daughter, Laurie, lay dying. I'd felt exiled from my wife and stepson to a living hell of doctors and CT scans and catheters and—most of all—hopelessness. I recalled attacks of heartburn that felt like heart attacks, and one afternoon getting lost trying to follow a winding corridor through the bowels of the hospital in search of an exit. I remembered the congregate of Christmas tree sellers I'd had to pass as the holiday approached and my growing anger and frustration at the commercialism surrounding the season.

All of which helped me see my daughter's suffering—her body pierced by four catheters, her labored breathing—as another crucifixion.

And I think now it was at that point my exile—my sense of being an outsider, a stranger in a strange land—became a pilgrimage, not in the sense of being reminded of my physical home in Maine, but of realizing that my emotional home, the origins of whatever faith I had in a higher power, grew from my suffering after Laurie died.

And since Jerusalem was the site not only of Jesus's crucifixion but also his resurrection, although I couldn't believe Jesus's molecules had miraculously reassembled themselves, I did believe he'd been resurrected in some form vivid enough for others to experience his presence, and that I wanted—no, needed—to believe my daughter had in some way been resurrected as well. And I saw that if I were going to believe this, I would find that belief, not in the Garden Tomb's quiet bucolic setting, but in a place like the Via Dolorosa—in heat and crowds of conflicting nationalities, soldiers and souvenir sellers, physical pain and taunting ridicule—where Jesus had suffered. Because this was like the place where Laurie had suffered.

Twenty-five years later, I'm still searching for that belief, that certainty. But the good news is that, over time, I've had more inklings of it—a sudden sense when I feel lost and confused that something or someone (God? Laurie?) is with me and knows the way. And I stumble on.

Joy and the Banjo

Linus to Charlie Brown: "I feel sorry for little babies.... When a little baby is born in this cold world, he's confused! He's frightened! He needs something to cheer him up.... The way I see it, as soon as a baby is born, he should be issued a banjo!"

IT WAS A DARK AND STORMY NIGHT. I SAT IN THE CHAPEL AND listened to the rain beat upon the windows and the wind blow through the trees. I was beginning a weekend retreat, called "Blowing Zen: Meditating with the Shakuhachi," run by the Society of Saint John the Evangelist, an Episcopal monastery in Massachusetts. I didn't know much about the shakuhachi except that it was a kind of flute. I was there because one of the facilitators of the retreat was Robert Jonas, who'd written a book about his daughter's death, *Rebecca: A Father's Journey from Grief to Gratitude*. A year or so earlier, I'd written to Jonas, as he prefers to be called, telling him how his book had helped me after my own daughter's death. He'd written back, we'd carried on a correspondence, and I wanted to meet him.

That first evening, Jonas and Martin Smith, Brother Superior at SSJE, both of whom played the shakuhachi, passed around several of the instruments and gave us a brief history lesson. Dating from the eighth century, the shakuhachi, or Zen flute, is made from bamboo root—hard as rock—and served as a weapon as well as a musical instrument for mendicant monks who wandered the countryside seeking enlightenment. These *komuso*, or "straw mat monks," considered the instrument a religious tool and gave primary attention to each breath-sound rather than to musical elements like melody. Their aim was to become, in the words of our handout, "a Buddha in one sound."

We ended the first evening in meditation, while Jonas played a song called "Crossing Over," which he said he had played at Rebecca's funeral. I sat on my Zen pillow, eyes closed, listening to the mournful tones of the flute mingled with the sounds of the wind and the rain and the wind chimes. (If you want to hear a shakuhachi, go to YouTube.) I focused on my breathing, and missed my daughter, Laurie, and wondered about what I would do with my life now that I was retiring from public school teaching, and missed Laurie some more. Then, suddenly, as Marlon Brando says in the movie *Apocalypse Now*, "…I realized…like I was shot…like I was shot with a diamond…a diamond bullet right through my forehead…."

I wanted to learn to play the banjo.

> *I come from Alabama with a banjo on my knee.*
> —Stephen Foster.

A month later, I'm walking into a music store in a rundown strip mall in Portland, Maine. Two guys in ripped, black T-shirts are behind the counter, and some kid with hair down to his ass is beating on an electric guitar. When I say I'm here for a banjo lesson, one of the guys behind the counter pinches some snuff from a round can, puts it under his lower lip, and points down a narrow aisle between racks of sheet music and guitar, mandolin, and banjo straps, picks, capos, and tuners. At the end of the aisle, I almost step on what looks for all the world like a pile of dog shit. And it is. A rubber pile of dog shit.

My first teacher is from West Virginia. Let's call him Gid. He smells of pot and body odor, and he says things like, "Hey, man! What's happenin'?" His three-month old daughter ("Man, was she a surprise!") sleeps in a guitar case beside us. Gid starts me on what's called claw-hammer style of playing, where my right hand is supposed to come down on the strings and hit the head of the banjo, almost as if I were knocking on a door. He is not so much concerned with my hitting the right notes as with establishing a rhythm. "Bounce, bounce!" he shouts, "Keep that rhythm going!"

I love it. Later, I will realize it's because of being totally focused, completely in the moment.

I'm goin' to a better world where everything is right…
where you never have to work at all or need to change your socks…
(American Folk Song)

Several years after I began playing the banjo, I went to Banjo Camp North in Massachusetts. While the weekend was set up in much in the same way as the spiritual retreats and writers' workshops I'd been going to—classes during the day, performances in the evening, informal get-togethers afterward—instead of the silence of the spiritual retreat or the intense, cerebral focus of the writing workshop, just about everyone at Banjo Camp was loose and laughing. It was impossible to tell the instructors—even some of the nationally known musicians—from the students. None of them sat at separate tables during meals. Like the rest of us, they talked about their kids and their bills and their clogged toilets.

The second afternoon, I attended a workshop called "Singing with the Banjo." I've always liked folk songs and figured we'd gather round and sing "Kumbaya" together. What I didn't expect was that we were all expected to solo. The closer it got to my turn, the more my hands and then my entire body trembled. I tried to pass, but Peggy Seeger, one of the famous Seegers of folk music, give me a pep talk about how she'd learned early in her career that she didn't have anything to prove, only something to share. So I shared my stage fright as I stumbled my way through a hobo song (see above lyrics), forgot some of the words, butchered the chords, but got through it.

We kept going on around the room until a woman—her voice quaking in fear—began her song. About halfway through, she stopped, started to cry, and ran from the building. I sought her out the next day to commiserate. Turned out, she was a journalist, and we agreed that writers—at least writers like us—were observers, not participants.

> *What a long strange trip it's been*—Jerry Garcia
> (Who, before he was a member of the Grateful Dead,
> played banjo for such groups as the Sleepy Hollow
> Stompers and the Thunder Mountain Tub Thumpers.)

Which, in a perverse sort of way, is why I've kept playing the banjo now for twenty-five years, performed with some local groups, even sung on occasion. For someone who spends the bulk of his time alone in front of a computer screen, who goes for silent walks in the woods, sits in silence gazing at his navel (although I prefer the term *omphaloskepsis*), and still daily misses his daughter, the instrument is a great antidote.

It's also a great instrument for pilgrimage. First made from an animal skin tacked over a hollowed half of a gourd, with three or four strings stretched over a planed stick, the "banza" or "banjar" came to this country from Africa with the slaves who played it in the same style that Gid taught me, and which I've stayed with. The banjo traveled across the country with settlers and around the world on whaling ships. (The banjo travels more easily than a guitar, as a matter of fact.)

The banjo also brings a little humor to the journey. It was a comic prop in minstrel shows, and banjo players remain the butt of any number of jokes. To wit:

> Q: What's the difference between playing a banjo and jumping on a trampoline?

A: You don't have to take your shoes off to jump on a trampoline.
Q: What do you call a banjo player who's just broken up with his girlfriend?
A: Homeless.

Like humor and like most of my favorite kinds of music (including the shakuhachi, the instrument of homeless, impoverished monks and at least one grieving parent, Robert Jonas), the banjo has its roots in sadness and loss yet blossoms in spontaneity and joy. In fact, I don't think I ever knew what joy was until I began whaling away on the banjo, knew that, unlike simple happiness or contentment or pleasure, joy contains the element of sadness, of longing.

The Christian writer C.S. Lewis defined joy as "an unsatisfied desire, which is itself more desirable than any satisfaction." I think what he's describing is similar to being on a pilgrimage: the desire is to reach a destination, but the joy comes from the journey.

I wonder if C.S. Lewis ever played the banjo.

Gifts

EVERY CHRISTMAS, I REMEMBER THAT THE MAGI—THOSE "WISE men from the East"—made one of the first pilgrimages, journeying to Bethlehem some two thousand years ago. They bore with them gifts of gold, frankincense, and myrrh, and ever since, giving gifts has been an indelible part of the Christmas season.

And every year, I realize once more how hard it is for me to receive a gift. How I feel I owe the giver something I'm not rich enough or clever enough or loving enough to repay, so that instead of making me grateful, the gift makes me feel second-rate, resentful.

I expect my problems with receiving gifts go back to my alcohol-fumed childhood. When he'd had enough to drink, my grandfather would try to give me one of his rifles or hunting knives. Usually, my mother would head him off at the pass, but I remember when he talked her into letting him give me a 7mm Mauser and then showed up the next week to take it back, only to give it to me again a year later.

Grampy's ex-wife, whom we called Nanny, always brought her grandchildren gifts when she visited. Sometimes, they were cheap, like the model airplane that broke the first time I flew it. Other times, she'd spend money she couldn't afford on presents such as a Hopalong Cassidy cap pistol in a genuine leather holster. Either way—when the wing fell off the plane or I heard Nanny tell Mom she couldn't pay her phone bill—I felt I was to blame. And no matter what the gift, I could never act happy enough. "Mmph. He must not like it," Nanny would say to Mom, as if I weren't standing between them. "I don't know why I bother. Nobody loves me."

Which probably explains why, of all the great spiritual teachings, the one I struggle the hardest with is grace. Christianity, Judaism, Buddhism, Hinduism, Taoism, and I expect other religious traditions all talk about grace, but it's the Christian concept that God loves us unconditionally that I grew up with and with which I struggle. At Christmas, I'm expected to believe that God became human solely out of love, not because of anything we'd done to earn that love.

Well, I'd rather believe "God helps those who help themselves." I'd rather be the transformed Scrooge, buying the biggest turkey in the market to give to Tiny Tim than I would Joseph, standing off to one side of the manger, welcoming a baby he hadn't fathered.

Ironically, it's been the death of my daughter that has helped me see—though dimly—how grace works. Like every parent who's ever lost a child, I suppose, I kept asking, "Why?" Why did my previously healthy daughter, who didn't drink or smoke—didn't even eat meat, for God's sake—die from this rare cancer?

Then, maybe ten years after Laurie died, I had coffee with a woman who'd recently watched her son die in a fire. The first thing she said to me was, "How have you survived?" I thought her question was extreme until I recalled Peter, whom I'd gotten to know a little when we were in grief counseling together (he'd also lost a daughter), who'd committed suicide earlier that year. Recently, I'd read about another grieving father who hanged himself in his garage.

How had I survived?

I recalled all the clergy, spiritual directors, and mentors who appeared unannounced in my life just when I needed them most. The way Mary Lee—whom I'd barely known when we decided to leave our spouses and live together, and who, by all logic, should have left me years earlier—stood by me. Why had these people appeared when they did? Why did Mary Lee remain? I had no more answers than I did for why Laurie died.

I think that's about the time I started thinking of God as "God of My Not Understanding."

Since then I've been better about being open to grace. Pilgrimages have helped. I think of Paul, a young priest in Jerusalem, who gave Mary Lee and me a personal tour of the Old City the first night we arrived; of an Agape service on the island of Iona in Scotland, where we shared raisins and water while a young man standing in an alcove in the ancient abbey played "Round Midnight" on a saxophone; of the large gray fox that visited us every night under a full moon at the Desert House of Prayer in Arizona.

But it's hard not to want to be more active. After all, I was raised to believe that real men *do* things.

Still, as I think of it, doesn't being open to grace also require activity? Let's look again at Joseph standing to one side of the manger. According to the story Christians tell each Christmas, it was only after he had defied the social code of his time and married his pregnant betrothed—when by rights he should have had her stoned to death—only after he led his by then nine-months-pregnant wife sixty-five miles (I looked it up) on a donkey and made her a birthing bed in some kind of animal enclosure that he was able to witness the grace of God.

Scrooge's turkey doesn't look so impressive anymore.

Thinking again about those years after Laurie died, I was not passive. I raged at God. Then, deciding that if I was going to spend all that time and energy yelling at God, I might as well listen to what God had to say back, I took up meditation, which, rather bringing me peace turned out to be twenty minutes of violent and upsetting images that I'd been repressing for years. I attended grief counseling. I worked with spiritual directors. I learned to ask for help. All of which, I'd say now, opened me to recognize and receive the love of God that had been there all along.

Gifts

I think of my little vegetable plot in our community garden. I find God's grace in the dirt and sun and rain that miraculously transform an inert seed into a string bean or a tomato. But those flowering plants won't do much flowering unless I prepare the soil, weed, mulch, and keep the various varmints away.

So, for me at least, the best way I can repay someone for their gift—whether it's from God of My Not Understanding or from Mary Lee's parents who gave us the money to add a second bathroom—is to receive it with gratitude.

The Path Is Made by Walking

Traveler, there is no path,
The path is made by walking.
—Antonio Machado

MENTION *PILGRIMAGE* AND FOLKS USUALLY THINK OF WALKING THE Santiago de Compostela or similar perambulations. Walking is synonymous with pilgrimage. In the Middle Ages, Chaucer's Canterbury pilgrims walked to the tomb of Thomas Becket, while serious pilgrims walked from Europe to the Holy City of Jerusalem. The practice of walking the labyrinth began then in order that older or more infirm pilgrims who couldn't make it to Jerusalem could at least take their own spiritual walk.

So maybe one reason I've come to see my life as a pilgrimage is that I've spent a large part of it walking.

As a kid growing up in Yarmouth, Maine, I walked to school, to the store, to the ball field, and to work. As an adult recovering from back surgery, I was told to walk ten miles a day for three months, which I did, even though those months were January, February, and March. After I moved back to Yarmouth, I began walking around town, one foot in the twenty-first century and one foot in 1955. Now living in Brunswick, Maine, I often walk the two miles to and from downtown, and the five miles of trails behind our house. I co-facilitate a contemplative silence group, where we practice not only sitting but also walking meditation: focusing on raising, lifting, pushing, dragging, touching, and pressing down each foot—to remind us that the body is always in the present moment.

* * *

Whenever I hear Johnny Mathis sing "Misty," I am immediately pulled back to an autumn Sunday in 1959, walking home from an afternoon with my first girlfriend. Floating was more like it, down Spring Street to East Main, to Willow, to Bridge Street, past white houses shaded by leaves shining ruby and golden in the sun, the smell of burning leaves like incense, buoyed by the taste of Susan's lips, the feel of her breast in my hand, the smell of her White Shoulders perfume, and the memory of Mathis's high tenor: "Oooonnnn my own, would I wander through this wonderland alone...." playing on her hi fi as we kissed.

On another Sunday, November 24, 1963, I walked through the evening mist and fog and the almost empty campus of the University of Maine at Orono, still in shock after the events of the weekend, which began with Walter Cronkite's voice: "From Dallas, Texas, the flash, apparently official: President Kennedy died at one p.m. Central Standard Time." I remember walking past Dunn Hall and Hannibal Hamlin and Oak Hall, standing like silent spectators at my one-man procession. The few remaining leaves of an oak tree hung like flags at half-staff. Evening mist turned to steady rain. I lit a cigarette and pulled the collar of my jacket around my neck. A feeling of loneliness such as I had never felt before—full of emptiness, longing, and sorrow—cascaded over me. I began to cry.

During the months of November and December of 1988, I walked a mile each way between the Ronald McDonald House in Bangor, Maine, to the fourth floor of the Eastern Maine Medical Center, where my eighteen-year-old daughter lay dying of cancer. I especially remember the walk back, through what I still think of as the bowels of the hospital. Confused and angry after a day by Laurie's bedside watching her slip further and further away from me, I'd take the elevator to the main lobby, walk through a waiting room, around a corner, and down a corridor lined at first with photographs of lighthouses and lobster boats, and then with memorial plaques hanging like rows of wooden shields along the wall. Head down, I walked past gray lockers, cinderblock walls, metal doors, laundry carts, baskets, and gurneys. Machines hummed. The lighting grew dimmer, the air damper. Pipes and valves clunked overhead. When I turned another corner into a still narrower corridor, the walls closed in on me, and it was here I sometimes heard voices of people walled up like victims in an Edgar Allen Poe short story, sensed ax murderers following me down the hall.

Just when it seemed the corridor would dead-end, a turn to the left led me to a narrow door, where I'd suddenly be excreted out into a parking lot by the river, the light, even on the darkest days, momentarily blinding me. But when my eyes adjusted to behold the cascading water and the russet oak trees and white birches on the riverbanks, their beauty was more painful than the ugliness I'd been living with for the previous six hours.

* * *

I used to love taking my grandchildren for walks in their strollers. Research has shown babies are happiest when they're carried while their parents, grandparents, or the like are walking at a speed of three to four miles an hour. So was at least one grandfather.

I've also found walking with them as they've grown older is a good reminder that, as Christine Valters Paintner writes, "Ultimately, the pilgrimage journey asks us…to relinquish our grasp on certainty and control." They go where they want, not where you want. Do you have someplace you need to be? Tough. Time does not exist.

But Valters Paintner goes on to explain, "In that process we allow ourselves…to receive gifts far bigger than our own limited imaginations could ponder." Amen. My grandchildren notice everything, and usually with a delight I'd long forgotten. What is more beautiful than a child's smile? More joyous than their laugh?

Most of the paths I've walked have been well-worn ones. I'm guessing most of you have also walked (if not physically, then emotionally) similar paths of love, sorrow, happiness, and grief. But I think each of us still has to find our own way forward along these paths—walk them as if they've never been walked before.

A Pilgrim's Journal: April 22, 1999

The Desert House of Prayer
Cortaro, Arizona

I SIT IN THE CHAPEL, WATCHING THROUGH A LARGE WINDOW BEHIND an altar the sun rise over saw-toothed mountains, splashing light over cactus—prickly pear, cholla, barrel, a saguaro—as well as sage, creosote, and mesquite bushes. The air is full of doves, cardinals, wrens, thrushes, and house finches. Just outside the window, a scrawny rabbit hops out of some sagebrush and down a path toward the guesthouses.

I've left Maine's mud season behind, but not my ongoing anxieties. Last night, as the wind rattled the windows and coyotes howled like elementary kids on a playground, I continued wrestling with God, with what I should do with my life after leaving the high school classroom—all compounded by the news of school shootings in Colorado.

I suppose the lesson here is that even on retreat, you can't escape the world. Yesterday I went for a walk through the Saguaro National Park, hiking along washes through red cliffs sentineled with saguaro, expecting any minute to run into John Wayne leading a cavalry troop and singing "She Wore a Yellow Ribbon," returning from my reverie to find Mary Lee in tears as she told me of the shooting of twenty-five high school students by two of their classmates. Violating my resolution to avoid reading the newspaper while on retreat, I read of the horror show that was Columbine, imagining the scene—the baggy pants, the hats worn backward—seeing I don't know how many students I've had over the past thirty years, either dead or wounded or pulling the trigger.

This morning, unable to sleep, I've come to the chapel to sit in front of the butcher block altar and the candles in their wrought-iron holders, to wait for seven o'clock and morning prayer and to look out the window and wait for some kind of answer, some kind of serenity.

The sun has crept over the mountains, setting the top of the giant saguaro aglow. All of a sudden, I'm not looking at a cactus in the desert, but at a birch tree swaying in the wind, and I'm sitting in front of another altar, staring through another window, this one overlooking the Penobscot River in Bangor, Maine.

I haven't spent a lot of time with my daughter this week. Oh, she's been here, sort of like the Arizona sky overhead, but two thousand miles away from home, wrestling with this other stuff, I haven't paid much attention to her. Now, however, I think of the November day a month or so before she died when I discovered the chapel in the Eastern Maine Medical Center.

It had been a particularly ugly day in Room 436. Laurie developed a fever of 102 degrees, Mary Lee's latest letter complained about bouncing a check, and I'd argued with my ex-wife, who wanted me to complain to our daughter's primary physician about one of the nurses.

When I left Laurie and her mother in the afternoon to go back to the Ronald McDonald House, I took the elevator as usual but, still upset about the day, got off on the wrong floor. Just as I realized my mistake, I found myself in front of a door marked with a small brass sign: "CHAPEL." I didn't know the hospital had one. Tentatively I turned the doorknob and walked in. The first thing I saw was a large round window framed by brown, gold, blue, and red glass behind the altar, looking out over the river. Along the riverbanks, a large birch tree metronomed in the wind. I felt as if I were looking at an animated stained-glass window.

I lit two pillar candles on the altar, sat down in the front row of chairs, and stared out the window at the rushing water. *This room seems so quiet,* I thought. Even in Laurie's single room at the end of the hall, there was always a steady undercurrent of noise from machines or voices in the hall or nearby TV sets. Here there was only the beating of my heart and the word *Why?* pounding in my head. Why couldn't anything be done to make my daughter more comfortable? Why did she have to get sick in the first place? Why was she dying?

I stared into the circle of stained glass. The window blurred. Wet flakes of snow lathered the glass, turning the circle white, scouring me to bone. The candles on either side of the altar seemed to glow more brightly, their light dancing. As I watched, the flames seemed to come together, enfolded by the stained glass around the white window. Then, I too become enfolded, and from somewhere I heard the words, "Don't ask why, just ask for help."

At first, I didn't realize what I'd heard. When I did, I became angry. *Okay, help,* I thought. *Help me make sense of this mess. Help me understand the reason for Laurie's pain and why she's going to die before she's ever really lived.*

But I couldn't take my eyes off the candles. From somewhere in the ceiling, fresh air cooled my face. I felt my body loosen. The stained glass seemed to keep drawing first my angry words and then all of me into its embrace.

"Don't ask why, just ask for help." The words didn't come from a *voice,* and they didn't come as any kind of epiphany—just a gentle, insistent, ever-deepening understanding, as if the words had always been there, but only now, in the silence of the chapel, could I hear them.

My sense of peace, of course, didn't last. When I returned to the hospital that evening, Laurie was vomiting dark-green bile. Although I began stopping regularly at the chapel after that, I didn't think much about the words I'd heard until after my daughter died.

Only now, over ten years later in Arizona, do I realize that "Don't ask why, just ask for help" is the only response I know to the death of a child, whether from cancer or from a bullet. I think of all the help I've received over the past ten years—from counselors, from clergy, from spiritual directors, from friends and family and especially Mary Lee, who may have kept me alive. And I wonder if it's now time for me to start thinking about trying to help others who have lost children. God knows I don't have much advice, but maybe just telling my story and listening to others tell theirs is enough.

So while I haven't been able to leave the past behind, coming to Arizona has given me a new perspective on that past—a new way to respond to it. I look again out the window at the giant saguaro cactus, standing with its arms upraised, as if in prayer or praise. Sometime this week, I learned that these cacti, which often live to be a hundred and fifty, even two hundred years old, don't start growing arms until they're sixty. Next week I'll be fifty-six. I've got time.

Waldo and Henry

SEVERAL YEARS AGO, WHEN MARY LEE AND I WERE GETTING READY to hike St. Cuthbert's Way, we drove over to our friendly L.L. Bean store and bought hiking poles. Now, Mary Lee had been using what she called walking sticks for at least ten years. Her doctor had recommended them to her as a way to build upper-body strength on her early morning walks and at the same time reduce wear and tear on her hips and back. While I thought what Mary Lee's doctor said might make sense for her, I never had any interest in the things. I didn't need any help walking, thank you very much, and, based on her experience, I didn't want to hear one more clown ask where my skis were.

But a sixty-two-mile hike was different, so we both bought adjustable hiking poles with these little shock-absorbers in them to provide further cushioning. They also have straps into which you insert your hands, one for the right hand and one for the left. Maybe because I don't have a lot of human friends and I'm not big on pets, I often name possessions. (My banjo, for example is "Joy," and our car is "Tembo," Swahili for elephant.) So I named my right hiking pole Waldo and the left one Henry.

Waldo is the name Ralph Waldo Emerson's friends called him. I'd recently read Robert D. Richardson Jr.'s book on Emerson called *The Mind on Fire*, which brought back memories of how important this nineteenth-century American philosopher and writer had been to me at one time. When I was teaching American literature and before I started attending church again, Emerson's essay "Nature" inspired me to take long Sunday afternoon walks through the woods of Down East Maine in search some kind of "spiritual" life, and I'm still more likely to feel in touch with the Holy in the woods or by the seashore or on a mountain than I am in the grandest cathedral. Later in my life, as I began to feel more and more tied down to a loveless marriage and a town I detested, Emerson's essay "Self-Reliance," with its emphasis on discovering one's true self and attaining independence, had helped give me the courage to leave both.

From *The Mind on Fire*, I learned that Emerson, often portrayed as the passionless "Sage of Concord," was a family man and a good neighbor whose life was marked by grief. His first wife had died at the age of twenty, and, after he remarried, his first son, Wallie, died from scarlet fever at the age of five. I resonated with the story that in the last hours of Emerson's life, forty years after his son's death, someone heard him whisper, "Oh, that beautiful boy!" As we grieving parents know, the grief never goes away, and when it hit me during our hike, it was helpful to have Waldo at my right hand.

One of Emerson's neighbors was Henry David Thoreau, whom Waldo befriended throughout Thoreau's life, hiring him to do odd jobs around the house, inviting him to dinner once a week, even during the two years that Henry was living what he portrayed in his classic book *Walden* as a solitary life on the shore of Walden Pond.

I first discovered Thoreau during what I call my "Kerouac years" in college, when I read his famous line, "The mass of men live lives of quiet desperation," thinking it described everyone but myself until those unhappy years in Down East Maine. After I fell in love with a woman from Colorado and met her in Boston for an October weekend in New England, we shared tins of sardines on the shore of Walden Pond, where I read to Mary Lee from *Walden*: "Go confidently in the direction of your dreams! Live the life you've imagined."

The Geriatric Pilgrim

Fifteen years or so after that, I took a retreat day and my tattered copy of *Walden* and drove to Concord, where I spent the day walking around Walden Pond, stopping periodically to read from the book and write in my journal. I got there early, and a morning mist hung over the water. I walked for a while and then sat on a rock, reading and staring out over what little water I could see. Out of the mist, a canoe appeared carrying two elderly—probably the age I am now—women. As they neared, sun parted the haze, highlighting the woman in the bow of the canoe: her plaid shirt and denim jeans, her lined and leathery face framed by a red hat and bandanna. I pulled out my journal and wrote how cool I thought it was that the women were so active at their age.

These days, I think it's even cooler.

* * *

I used Waldo and Henry on our trek through Scotland and England, and found, as Mary Lee's doctor had said, how much easier it was to walk with them. They gave me a boost up the hills. They supported me on the way down. Several times they kept me from falling into the mud. I found myself talking to them, which isn't that unusual. I not only name inanimate objects, I talk to them (especially recalcitrant jar covers—*Come on, damn you, open!*), but I also discovered I was listening to what they had to say back—*Okay, slow down here....Come on, you can make it up this hill. Move!*

Since then, Waldo and Henry have accompanied me on hikes through the saguaro in Arizona, along the rocky coast of Maine, through the poison ivy along the riverbanks in Massachusetts, and through the Black Forest in Germany. I've given them baskets to use when I go snowshoeing. They've come to symbolize a spirit of adventure, of pilgrimage. (After all, most images of pilgrimage show the pilgrim with a staff. The trouble is, a staff throws my back out.)

A couple of years ago, I started using Waldo and Henry after winter storms to keep me and my increasingly fragile bones from breaking.

Now I'm using them almost all the time for my walks. In winter, I can say it's because of the ice, but the fact is I just feel better when I use them. I don't have to soak my back after walking. My knees don't ache. So as much as I hate to say it, Waldo and Henry are coming to represent my aging body. I notice people at church using hiking poles to get up and down the aisles, and I see my future.

They also indicate my need for help, my need to admit that I'm not as independent as I like to think I am. The irony is that I'm more confident in who I am, less concerned with what other people think about me. When I hear, "Where are your skis?" I smile and say, "Oh, I knew I forgot something."

In some ways, then, I've become more self-reliant. I think the real Waldo and Henry would like that.

Healed Doesn't Mean Cured

Pilgrimage is...an act of devotion to find a source of healing....
—Phillip Cousineau, *The Art of the Pilgrimage*

RIGHT AFTER MY PARENTS BOUGHT OUR FIRST TELEVISION SET IN 1953, our family watched everything from test patterns to evangelist Oral Roberts sitting in a tent, healing people's various medical misfortunes: tuberculosis, speech impediments, polio ("Praise God, Billy Ray, I can feel the stiffness leaving your little foot!")—you name it. Since my father was skeptical (he said the show was a crock of shit), I too doubted the healing power of prayer.

But I was never strongly opposed to the idea that faith can cure disease and other afflictions until my daughter was diagnosed with cancer. The object of my most intense anger was not TV evangelism but the alternative health industry. I recall sitting by Laurie's bedside in the hospital, reading ads to her from a glossy magazine she subscribed to for Royal Jelly, Ayurvedic Ginseng, and macrobiotic hair care, "Refreshing Summer Seaweeds," "Nontoxic Alternatives to Mercury Fillings," and "Curing Infertility through Chinese Medicine."

One afternoon, she wanted me to read an article entitled "Alternative Cures for Cancer." The gist of the article was that, rather than deadly chemicals and mind-altering drugs, the best way to cure cancer is with a healthy, positive self-image built on faith and love. I think the article posited that 80 to 90 percent of all cancer is preventable.

At some point while I was reading, I heard a thick voice slurred by morphine: "I've tried…to be positive…but I guess I'm just not strong enough…I wish I weren't such a wimp."

Her words still haunt me. Bad enough that my daughter had to die, but for her to feel that it was somehow her fault because she didn't have enough faith fills me with rage. Over the thirty-four years since Laurie's death, I have walked out of a teacher workshop on "Wellness" in order to write angry letters to my principal and superintendent on the dangers of trying to teach what I saw as unrealistic expectations. I have seethed at Biblical stories of Jesus bringing some people back to life, while others die. And I remember grinding my teeth after 9/11 when a parishioner at the church I attend publicly thanked God for saving her son who worked in one of the twin towers.

"What about the other three thousand who died?" I muttered to Mary Lee. "What did God have against them?"

My attitude began to change, however, after Mary Lee and I attended a healing service on the island of Iona in Scotland. The pastor began by saying we need to remember that healing doesn't mean curing. The word *heal*, he said, comes from the word *whole*, and he believed that God's purpose for us all is a life of wholeness. The healing service, then, was not about changing God, but about learning to trust God, even as we don't know when or how or what kind of healing will happen.

Gradually—very gradually—I've begun to understand his distinction. For example, when Mary Lee and I started training for our pilgrimage along Saint Cuthbert's Way, we both experienced back, hip, hamstring, calf, ankle, and foot pain. I have two artificial hips. The latest CT scan of my back has revealed severe narrowing of the lower thoracic disks, "vacuum disc phenomenon," severe narrowing of L2-L3 disc, "degenerative hypertrophic bone," "mild compression, mild spinal stenosis, ossification, [and] lower lumbar facet degenerative disease."

I'm not sure what all that means, but I do know I'm four inches shorter than I was in high school. Mary Lee has had her right foot completely reconstructed. One of her shoulders is higher than the other because of scoliosis, and she has suffered from allergies and thyroid trouble.

And you know what? After walking the sixty-two miles of Saint Cuthbert's Way, we still hurt. Neither my back nor Mary Lee's miraculously straightened. My wife's allergies didn't go away. No amount of walking could cure the fatal disease of being human.

And yet, we returned from our pilgrimage feeling more than the rejuvenation one feels when returning from a vacation or even from most of our retreats. We've bought bicycles, climbed a few small mountains, and taken up snowshoeing. I've tried to incorporate some of the walking meditation I practiced along St. Cuthbert's Way, not only into my daily walks around town, but also into washing dishes, vacuuming the floors, and sitting through this country's political mud-slinging.

I think distinguishing between being cured and being healed is even more important when talking about grief. Over the years, a number of people have asked me if the pain of losing Laurie has become less. My answer lately is that my grief isn't any less, but it's less important. I still cry when I think of my daughter, I'm still angry at God for creating a world in which innocent children suffer and die, and I still sometimes feel irrationally responsible for her death, either because of what I did or what I didn't do.

But at the same time, I am no longer consumed by anguish. I no longer base my identity on being Grieving Parent. My sadness, anger, and guilt have become enveloped, maybe even embraced, by something larger. I am perhaps more whole now than I have ever been, even though I'm not cured of wanting to watch my daughter become an adult, talking to her on the phone, or seeing her interact with my grandchildren, maybe even with children of her own.

Hell, I'm not cured of wishing I were six foot two again.

Edu-cations

THE OTHER DAY, I WAS TRYING TO CONSOLIDATE PHOTOS ON MY computer (does anyone besides me miss the old photograph albums?) when I found around a hundred pictures from August of 2009 when Mary Lee and I participated in a Stonecoast in Ireland writing program. Looking at the slideshow I created (okay, computers have their advantages), I realized I've never thought of my week in Dingle on the southwest coast of Ireland as a pilgrimage. At the same time, it wasn't a vacation.

I decided the best word to describe it would be an *edu-cation.*

Now there were certainly elements of a vacation. Our program leaders, Ted and Annie Deppe (both fine poets, teachers, and really cool people—check out their work), had planned each day: mornings devoted to each participant's teaching a class on a writer they admired, critiquing the essays, fiction, and poetry we'd submitted (I'd never been in a mixed genre workshop before), and listening to guest lecturers; afternoons and evenings eating in Dingle's fine restaurants and listening to Irish jigs and reels in the pubs, and being chauffeured and guided around southwestern Ireland in style.

Dingle is a town geared for those on vacation. In addition to all the places to eat and drink, there are gift shops, a lovely bookstore (where we did a reading one night), woolen shops, and an aquarium. Walking the streets, I heard German, British, Italian, French, and Japanese, as well as American, accents. The week I was there, Dingle harbor was full of yachts for some regatta. Tour boats took passengers out to catch a glimpse of Fungi, a beloved dolphin who'd been a tourist attraction since the 1980s. The Coastline Motel, where we stayed and had our classes, was comfortable, and the breakfasts were scrumptious.

On the other hand, pilgrimages are supposed to be difficult, and traveling to Ireland was more difficult than any pilgrimage I've been on. When Mary Lee and I put together our trip, we wanted some retreat time, so we booked our first night in Ireland a day early in Glenstal Abbey outside of Limerick. Due to thunderstorms and something called "pilot time," however, we spent the first night of our trip in Saugus, Massachusetts. (To help me write this reflection, I put on the Skyteam T-shirt I still have from Delta's overnight bag.) On the day we'd planned to be in silence and slow time at Glenstal Abbey, we spent thirteen hours in Kennedy Airport in New York City, trying to find an internet connection so that I could explain to the brothers why we weren't there (they were very nice and didn't charge us), running back and forth from one end of the terminal to the other because the plane to Shannon Airport kept changing gates, and listening to people screaming at ticket agents in eighty-seven different languages. (If someday for my sins I go to Hell, I expect it will be a lot like Kennedy Airport.)

The other challenging trip was to Great Blasket Island, three miles off Ireland's western coast. Because of weather conditions, we didn't know when we were going, and the trip we did make came at the last minute, when the captain of our tour boat saw "a window of opportunity." (This, I found out later, meant the ocean swells had dropped from twenty feet to six to ten feet.) In a steady rain, we boarded the boat and chugged to the island, where we transferred to motorized rubber rafts to go ashore.

Once on the island, I entered the same kind of liminal space I've mentioned before. Empty windows of stone houses peered at me from the furze and heather growing on peat bogs. Wild sheep and donkeys grazed, and rabbits scampered across footpaths. The island was abandoned in 1953, but before then, it had been inhabited since the sixteenth century, and by the early 1700s, there had been as many as 170 people fishing and farming there. The reason Ted and Annie included this trip in the itinerary was because in the 1920s and '30s, Great Blasket Island was known for its writers, publishing in the native Irish language about life on the edge of European civilization. But after that, the population continued to decline until there was no one left.

By the time we disembarked from our rubber rafts, the rain was coming down hard. Good Mainers that we are, Mary Lee and I had our L.L. Bean raingear and waterproof hiking boots, so we took off for the northern part of the island, past the houses and the sheep, splashing through mud puddles and a bog that seemed to be breathing.

My wife was in heaven. In her other life (our term for the years before we met), she'd owned a donkey, and she thinks of the donkey as her spirit animal. She immediately gravitated to those descendants of the work animals islanders used instead of horses.

I was more interested in the views of the water and the fifteen seals bobbing up and down like kids waiting for the movie theater to open, and the melancholic sense of standing on the soggy, uneven ground between life—Mary Lee petting the donkeys, the seals below me, the seabirds circling overhead—and death, symbolized by the collapsed stone houses.

Great Blasket was not a "spiritual" destination as such. Although I gather monks lived here in the sixteenth and seventeenth centuries, there were no monastic ruins, not even a cemetery (when someone died, they were taken to the mainland for burial). Unlike most of my pilgrimages, there was nobody in particular I had made this journey to honor.

Still, as far as I'm concerned, the day was a spiritual experience.

Which raises the old question: what does *spiritual* mean? Writers on pilgrimage often refer to "the call to pilgrimage," a longing to reach a destination, one connected with a destination within yourself, one that ties you to the transcendent. One of the reasons I wanted to participate in Stonecoast in Ireland, was that I yearned for my writing to be published and to fulfill a vow I'd made to Laurie after she died to become a writer as a way to honor her memory. (And the essay I took with me to Ireland was eventually published as part of my novel *Requiem in Stones*.)

I was also paying homage to writers I admire and want to emulate. I made a presentation to my class on Frank McCourt, one of my literary heroes, both because he was a former high school English teacher and because he didn't publish his first book, *Angela's Ashes*, until he was in his late sixties.

So while the call to make this trip probably wasn't spiritual in the sense of my trying to become closer to God, it wasn't simply to get away, either. My edu-cation to Dingle became an interior journey to creative parts of myself I didn't know were there. I began writing poetry. I developed a love of Irish music. I made friendships that continue to this day.

Edu-cations show me how blurred the line between pilgrimage and vacation can be. Which reveals the blurred line between spiritual and secular.

More and more, I'm coming to believe that no matter how they begin, my real pilgrimages are the journeys I make through the landscapes—the bogs and ocean views, the empty houses and spirit animals, the loud conflicts and lilting music (not to mention the digressions that keep pulling me off track)—of myself.

The Dark Woods

I'M LOOKING OUT THE WINDOW AT A GRAY DAY, THINKING OF A GRAY September day when Mary Lee and I crossed over the stile between Scotland and England on our walking pilgrimage of St. Cuthbert's Way. I recall being disappointed that Mel Gibson as William Wallace, his face painted blue, didn't come out of the mist to check our passports, but I did notice, as we hiked down a grassy hill toward what my map told me was Elsdon Burn, the grass was longer—something to do with different grazing laws in England—and felt the excitement and satisfaction of having walked from one country into another.

But I also remember that at the foot of the hill, the ground became boggy, and my enthusiasm faded. When Mary Lee and I crossed a stream and started up a gradual incline, I was aware of my lungs working harder. My feet were covered with moleskin to protect them from blisters, but I could feel several hot spots as well as a vague soreness in my right Achilles tendon. I thought about how that day was our longest leg of the pilgrimage, fourteen miles, and how worried I was that we wouldn't make it to our next B&B by dark. I'd turned seventy. My mother had died earlier that year. Instead of paying attention to the grazing sheep and the mist on my face and the smells of grass and earth, thoughts of mortality clung like the mud on my hiking boots.

Then, ahead of me, I saw the Dark Woods.

The Geriatric Pilgrim

Almost all our hiking had been through open fields, and when we had walked through trees, they'd been tall and widely spaced apart. This looked like a plantation of closely spaced fir. As Mary Lee and I stood in front of the entrance, the path snaked into a blackness that mirrored my mood.

I think I'm remembering that day because today I'm in a similar frame of mind. I'm writing this in the darkest time of the year, when we get, if the sun stays out all day (and it seldom does), nine hours of light. After a delightful Thanksgiving with all the grandchildren, I'm now waking up in the middle of the night, worried about a pandemic that's threatening their education, let alone God-knows-what-else in their lives, and a country that seems hell-bent on destruction; reliving the last two months of my daughter's life; and, after heart surgery and a recent diagnosis of "moderate" COPD, pondering my mortality.

Ever the old literature teacher, I think of F. Scott Fitzgerald writing of "…a real dark night of the soul, [where] it is always three o'clock in the morning.…" Recalling those woods on St. Cuthbert's way, I recall the "Dark Wood of Error" in Dante's *Inferno*, which, if I remember correctly, stood for the protagonist's physical, psychological, and spiritual ignorance. Unlike Dante's character, however, who soon left the Dark Wood behind to begin his linear pilgrimage through Hell, Purgatory, and Heaven, I've circled through any number of Dark Woods of Error. My life is a litany of stupid decisions: an unhappy and largely wasted four years of college, a poor marriage, money frittered away, precious time—time I could have spent with my daughter—wasted.

But then I recall that when Mary Lee and I ducked our head through the first low branches and entered the forest, I heard her say, "What a strange and interesting place." And it hit me, and it hits me now, that I'd rather be in the Dark Wood of Error with her than anyplace else I can think of without her. That after Laurie died, she held me together with her quiet strength, deep wisdom, and unwavering love. And still does. I'm given to exaggerating, but I'm honestly not sure I'd be alive today if she hadn't been by my side through those black nights.

As it turned out, those dark woods along St. Cuthbert's Way turned out to be a fascinating interlude, completely different from any other landscape we experienced on that pilgrimage. And I'm suddenly wondering if darkness is always such a bad place.

More memories: I'm four years old, climbing into a cabinet in the living room of the house I grew up in and nestling in the warm, comforting darkness next to the chimney. I'm six, burrowing under the covers of my bed, listening to *Bobby Benson and the B-Bar-B Riders* on the radio. I'm nine, and I'm sick, and my mother enfolds me into the soft dark of her bosom.

Most of what I euphemistically call my "spiritual life," I realize, is fed by the silence and darkness of my meditation practice, which, along with Mary Lee's love, I credit for helping me resurrect my life after my daughter's death. Thinking again of that phrase, "the dark night of the soul," I remind myself that Fitzgerald took the term from the Spanish mystic, St. John of the Cross, who considered this spiritual suffering necessary if we are to be liberated by God from our preoccupation with ourselves and our experiences.

So what's the difference between being in the Dark Wood of Error, the darkness of ignorance, and living in what an anonymous fourteenth-century monk called "The Cloud of Unknowing," which he suggested was the place for spiritual practice? The first is, in my experience, disorienting, unplanned, unwanted. I thrash around, fearful and frustrated, a slave to my emotions and my ego. The second is a place I've chosen to be, like meditation or those woods, one in which I surrender and where sometimes, I experience the freedom of not knowing, but of being known and loved.

I'm suddenly thinking I need to ask Mary Lee if she wants to go for a walk in the woods behind our house.

Some Stones from the Journey

Go inside a stone,
That would be my way....
—Charles Simic

As a way to retain some of the pilgrimage experience, I collect stones. I'm not talking just a few stones here; I'm talking bowls of stones in almost every room of the house. Fountains of stones. Stone paper weights and bookends. Stones too large for the house lining the back patio.

* * *

Before I ever thought much about pilgrimages, my then twelve-year-old daughter, Laurie, gave me a "rock concert" for Father's Day: a dozen small stones she'd painted blue and red and arranged in clay on a wooden oval. She painted black-and-white eyes like a raccoon's on each stone, a nice touch, typical of her attention to detail.

You can also see her attention to detail in the watercolor she painted when she was seventeen. In the center of the picture, a pale turquoise hand reaches up through large greenish-brown stones toward a diaphanous orange petal drifting down from a cluster of flower blossoms. Laurie gave me this painting before her cancer diagnosis, when her future seemed bright and limitless, but after her death I spent hours sitting in front of that watercolor, feeling the desperation embodied in the hand as it reaches for one fragile blossom of beauty before being crushed under the weight of those stones.

* * *

According to Hasidic legend, after Moses came down from Mount Sinai with the Ten Commandments carved on stone tablets and saw the children of Israel worshipping a golden calf, he smashed the tablets to the ground, leaving behind a pile of stone fragments. The people, unable to bear leaving the pieces there, picked them up and carried them in their pockets all through their desert wanderings toward the home they were hoping to find.

* * *

When my wife, her son, and I decided it was time to "graduate" from the Center for Grieving Children, a local organization offering counseling to families who've lost loved ones, we each received a leather pouch containing four stones. Three were round and smooth, representing "the bright and shiny parts of you, the parts that have healed and grown and are stronger than before." One was flat and rough, "like the corner of your heart that may always feel a little rough and painful because of what's happened to you." I carried that stone for years. Sometimes, when I was tearful or angry or felt especially guilty for Laurie's death because of what I had or hadn't done, it felt good to grip the stone tightly so the edges cut into the palm of my hand. The surface of the stone was cracked and pitted, and sometimes I'd dig with my thumbnail into the crevices. That was very satisfying.

* * *

Jungians talk about a "collective unconscious," a mental package of instinctual feelings passed down from life's beginnings. Perhaps,

Robert M. Thorson, postulates in his book on New England stone walls, *Stone by Stone*, we all carry with us a primitive need for stones as the material for tools and weapons, as shelters for homes, as natural enclosures into which to drive game, as caches for hiding food, or as places for ambush or escape.

* * *

For years after my daughter's death, I dreamed of long, lopsided stones, smoke colored. Sometimes they lay on their sides. Sometimes they fit together in a wall or a house. Sometimes they were in the rubble of destroyed cities. Sometimes they were standing, and I used them to navigate my way through the wilderness.

* * *

Thorson explains that we imbibe stones every day because, unless artificially distilled, all the earth's water carries with it the dissolved constituents of stones. So in a way, we are all built of stones.

* * *

During a trip to England, the year after Laurie died, Mary Lee bought me a stone from Salisbury Cathedral. It's a block of ash-gray limestone, about two inches wide, four inches long, and three-quarters of an inch thick. On the back, there's a "Certificate of Authenticity," part of which reads:

> ...*centuries of storm and frost, and, more recently, the deadly corrosion of acid rain, have eaten the medieval stonework away. This fragment is a genuine piece of the original masonry removed from the spire, to be replaced with fresh stone from the same quarry.*

When we arrived at Salisbury Cathedral, I was disappointed to see the famous spire encased in scaffolding. Holding Mary Lee's gift, however, comforted me with the knowledge that this ancient stone monument to both God and the human spirit needed to be—and could be—repaired, offering hope that I might do the same with my own life.

* * *

One of the Jewish names for God is "The Rock of Israel." Christianity's Saint Peter (from *petros*, meaning "rock") talks about Jesus as the "stone that was rejected" becoming the chief cornerstone in the new house of faith.

* * *

After climbing the Mount of Olives, across the Kidron Valley from the Old City of Jerusalem, Mary Lee and I descended through a huge Jewish cemetery of low, flat stone vaults made of cream-colored limestone called Jerusalem stone, used for centuries in buildings and walls. Instead of flowers, relatives decorate the tops of these graves with small chunks of Jerusalem stone—perhaps as a religious tribute to the presence of God the Rock, perhaps as a secular way to show respect, or perhaps as a superstition that the added stones help the souls of the dead stay put in their new homes—no one apparently really knows why. What I do know is that I went back to our guest house that night with my pockets weighed down with Jerusalem stone to place on my daughter's memorial stone in our family's cemetery.

* * *

Some of the stones on the Scottish island of Iona are over three billion years old. They have seen the formation of continents, the rise and fall of mountain ranges, several reversals of the magnetic poles, and at least five mass extinctions of the world's species.

They are also alive. Geologists tell us that if we were able—as Charles Simic would like—to go inside a stone, we'd find that it consists of elements made up of plus and minus charges, negative electrons circling protons like tiny solar systems. So that, far from being dead and inert—stone cold, a heart of stone—stones are full of energy.

This doesn't surprise me. There's a primordial power, a mysterious force in stones that has often made me wonder whether, instead of my collecting all these stones over the years, these stones haven't been collecting me.

Baseball as Pilgrimage

EVERY YEAR, MILLIONS OF PEOPLE MAKE A PILGRIMAGE TO SEE THEIR favorite baseball team. I'm sure most of them don't think of taking in a ball game as pilgrimage, but, as with all pilgrimages, going to a game often involves, at some level, making a journey that is both physical and spiritual, taking risks, paying homage, and searching for a source of healing and renewal.

It's possible, then, that the first pilgrimage I ever took was to Fenway Park in 1954 to see the Red Sox play the Detroit Tigers. I remember the ride to and from Boston was interminable; Fenway Park was huge; Red Sox first baseman, Harry Agganis (who would die a year later of a pulmonary embolism), looked like a god; and I ate lobster at a restaurant on the ride back, courtesy of my little league coach, Frank Knight (who would live to be 103).

I was reminded of my early love of baseball recently when I read *Dingers: The 101 Most Memorable Home Runs in Baseball History* by Joshua Shifrin and Tommy Shea. I've had the good fortune to have shared a number of cups of coffee and conversation with Tommy Shea, who was a reporter for the *Springfield* (Massachusetts) *Republican* for forty years, including six years covering the Red Sox, and whose very being exudes the joy I once felt about the game. (Nobody's perfect, however; Tommy is a Yankees fan.)

The Geriatric Pilgrim

* * *

I hit two dingers in my baseball career. The first, in little league, cleared the fence and almost hit my family's car. The second, when I was in the eighth grade, disappeared into the fog blowing in off Cape Elizabeth, Maine, but since there was no fence, I had to run it out. I run like a wheelbarrow, so I barely beat the throw home. Still, I thought I had won our team the game, until Ronnie Bancroft, the Cape third baseman, tagged me after I'd crossed the plate, and the umpire called me out. "Sorry, son," he said, "but your foot missed third base by a good two feet." (For those of you who don't know much about baseball, the runner must touch every bag before touching home plate.)

So much for my making it into Shifrin's and Shea's book.

But one of the home runs that did make it into the book—Shifrin and Shea rank it as the fifth most memorable home run in baseball history—is Kirk Gibson's game-winning home run in the 1988 World Series against Hall of Fame relief pitcher Dennis Eckersley. In fact, *Dingers* features on its cover what has become an iconic picture of Gibson, hand raised over his head in victory.

I remember Gibson's home run even more than I remember my own. His took place on the October weekend when Mary Lee and I were visiting my daughter, Laurie, in Ellsworth, Maine. That spring, Laurie had been diagnosed with cancer. Over the summer, chemotherapy and radiation had shrunk the tumor, and we were hopeful, but in September, while she was walking a beach, her leg collapsed under her, and since that time, she'd needed to use a walker. In continuous pain, Laurie was trying to remain positive, living at home with her mother, working on various art projects, and designing placemats for a new restaurant in town, but she was discouraged and fearful, often dissolving in tears as she talked with me on the phone. To give both Laurie and my ex-wife a break, Mary Lee and I drove up for the weekend, rented a motel room, and took Laurie to stay with us.

On Saturday afternoon, we drove around Hancock County looking at foliage until a freak snowstorm sent us back to our motel. That evening we went to the new restaurant that featured Laurie's placemats, but my daughter's leg pain grew so bad that we couldn't finish our meal. Mary Lee and I had to carry her out to the car.

Back at the motel, Laurie lay down on our bed, closed her eyes, and, I thought, fell asleep. I turned on the television just in time to see Gibson, of the Los Angeles Dodgers, who hadn't been in the game because of a severely strained hamstring in one leg and a bad knee in the other, come to the plate as a pinch hitter. The Dodgers were behind the Oakland Athletics by one run in the bottom of the ninth inning. They had a man on first base, but there were two outs. With a count of three balls and two strikes, Gibson, with what Shifrin and Shea describe as "an awkward upper-body swipe," hit his home run. As he limped around the bases, pumping his fist, and one talking head after another extolled his courage in the face of pain, I heard Laurie say to Mary Lee, who lay beside her on the bed, "I know this cancer might—probably will—kill me, but hopefully not for years. I need to make the most of whatever time I've got left."

I looked at my daughter, her bright red bandanna and matching socks, her eyes sunken, her face drawn by pain. *Those idiots on TV have no idea what courage is,* I thought bitterly.

And there's part of me that still feels that way. I'm certainly not the first person to complain about how we have glorified sports beyond reason and deified grown people playing games. But like pilgrimage, sports—and I would say especially baseball—is a way to encapsulate the human journey in a few hours. We fans travel to what one of my favorite movies calls our "field of dreams," and the players themselves try to get, as we all do, "home," where, as James Earl Jones says in the film, "…what once was good…will be again."

Home is where my daughter went less than three months after Gibson's dramatic "dinger." Now that I'm eighty, it helps to see myself rounding third base (making sure to touch it this time), heading to join her.

The Fugitive in the Photo

According to the journal I kept for our first trip outside the United States, this photograph was taken on Saturday, July 21, 1990. The place is Stratford-upon-Avon, and the guy is standing in front of Shakespeare's birthplace. His wife, Mary Lee, (who snapped the picture) and he are in England, taking a summer program called Shakespeare's World. That evening, along with the rest of their winter teacher/summer student classmates, they'll watch the Royal Shakespeare Company's production of *Much Ado About Nothing* before getting on the bus and returning to Cambridge University for another week of classes.

When I first looked at the man in this photograph, I noticed our similar tastes. We both like hats (not crazy about the one he's wearing, but he likes it), we both prefer chinos to blue jeans, and we both keep a notebook in our shirt pocket. Although the snappy cap and the camera suggest he's a tourist, he, like me, hates identifying himself this way, maybe because we both grew up in Maine, "Vacationland," where we learned to disdain the visitors we called "summer complaints."

As I continued looking at the photograph, I noticed differences between this man and me, some of which only I would know. For example, he's taller than I am by several inches, and his face is freer of wrinkles, lines, and age spots. He doesn't have a fatty lump on his back. He's got a beard, which as I remember, grows and wanes almost as often as the moon. Same with his hair, which I don't have much of now.

When I came upon my journal entries, I was hoping to discover that this guy's trip to Stratford foreshadowed the way I think of myself these days: as a pilgrim. After all, what English teacher wouldn't want to make a pilgrimage to Shakespeare's birthplace? But deep down, I knew words like *pilgrim* and *pilgrimage* weren't part of his vocabulary. He and Mary Lee have just decided not to stand in the long line going into the house. He'd much rather leave, watch some street entertainers, and get another pint at a nearby pub called the Slug and Lettuce.

No, the man thinks of himself as a teacher, not a pilgrim. After all, teaching has been the only fulltime job he's ever held, and he's been doing it for twenty-five years. Writers are his heroes, and watching a student's eyes light up when he's able to connect him or her to *Macbeth* or *Romeo and Juliet* is what's fed him all these years. When he and Mary Lee were looking at travel opportunities, they chose an academic program—as they wrote in their applications to their respective school boards for continuing education credits—to improve their teaching.

The Geriatric Pilgrim

The problem is the man in the photograph is not sure he wants to teach anymore. Certainly not in high school, where his seventeen- and eighteen-year-old students remind him of his daughter, who died a year and a half earlier. He has no patience with their excuses, their backtalk, their acting up. "Why are you alive," he wants to yell sometimes, "and my brilliant, sensitive, compassionate daughter is dead?"

The truth is that what this man wants to do this summer is escape from his pain. The more I gazed into the photograph, the more clearly I saw a pale, halting, self-conscious man, picking at his camera strap as if it's part of a straitjacket, waving his arm as if he wants to fly away.

Except he has no idea which direction he wants to go.

* * *

Dictionary.com defines *fugitive* as "a person who is fleeing from prosecution or intolerable circumstances." Both are true of this man. Since his daughter's death a year and a half earlier, he has prosecuted himself mercilessly, convinced that his divorce and remarriage caused his daughter's cancer. And life has become, if not intolerable, then unpleasant—a wary, static existence, punctuated by waves of pain, less frequent than before but, as a result, more unexpected, stronger. He and his wife eye each other warily from behind their respective barricades, as careful with their words as with sticks of dynamite, afraid some careless comment might light the fuse and blow their marriage to pieces.

Besides trying to get away from his students, his unhappy home life, and his guilt, he's also trying to flee God. At least, the God of his understanding: a super sadist, who gets his kicks torturing innocent eighteen-year-old girls. It would be easier if he didn't believe in God, but he's tried that, and he can't. So, he alternates between raging at God and running away, like Jonah, the Hebrew prophet who tried to flee God and was swallowed by "a great fish."

And, like Jonah, he's finding out one cannot escape the past. Three weeks into the program, his wife misses her two sons spending the

The Fugitive in the Photo

summer with their father in Colorado. She's upset that, because of the time difference, she hasn't been able to talk to them on the phone. Which always triggers this nasty voice in his head: "Well, they're alive, aren't they?"

He's sick of feeling the stab in his heart from the question, "How many children do you and your wife have?" And when one woman in the program looks at a photograph of his wife's son and remarks on how much Jeremy looks like both Mary Lee and him, he thinks he might barf up his Green King Ale. Instead of Shakespeare, he keeps hearing F. Scott Fitzgerald: "So we beat on, boats against the current, borne back ceaselessly into the past."

While I feel sorry for the fugitive in the photograph, I also want to tell him he will return from England carrying the seeds of his rebirth. Part of the Shakespeare program is to visit English cathedrals, and by the time he leaves England, he will have spent time in St. Benedict's, King's College Cathedral, and St. John's College Cathedral in Cambridge, Salisbury Cathedral, St. Mary's in Bath, Peterborough Cathedral, Ely Cathedral, and Holy Trinity Church in Stratford. Because for most people these days, these are historical rather than spiritual sites, he won't connect them with his anger and fear of God; rather, he will find in these old cathedrals a certain peace as well as a crumb of hope. He will see ancient buildings comprised of more ancient stones, created by a confluence of spirit, sweat, intellect, and prayer. Many of these cathedrals are in a state of continual renovation, and he will start to wonder whether the fact that these ancient stone monuments to God and the human spirit need to be—and can be—periodically repaired may offer hope that he can rebuild his *own* life.

Returning to Maine, recalling these three weeks, he will take away from these remodeled cathedrals a need to come up with not only a goal, but also a blueprint for getting there. The following fall, he will learn about Centering Prayer, a form of Christian meditation which becomes his handbook of instructions for not running from his fears, but simply to watch them, watch himself react, and then let the fears go. He will, in the words of the 12-step program he will join, "Let go and let God." Not God the Super Sadist, but God the Great Embrace.

My journal tells me that after Mary Lee took this picture, they walked through the park by the River Avon to Trinity Church, where Shakespeare is buried. The church, like everywhere else in Stratford, was full of people, but, I write, the mood was far less frenetic. That's because (and I quote from my journal), "…as Mary Lee said, they were pilgrims, not tourists."

I'm pretty sure this was the first time I ever heard anyone I knew talk about someone's trip being a pilgrimage.

It was certainly not the last.

A Pilgrim's Journal: August 9, 2002

Iona, Scotland

ON WHAT WOULD HAVE BEEN LAURIE'S THIRTY-SECOND BIRTHDAY, I sit on a ledge by the shore of Columba's Bay. Waves break on the rocks, ethereal light shimmers around me, and huge white clouds lie low over the water. Some fifteen hundred years ago, an Irish monk landed on this shore with twelve brothers and established the monastery in which Western Christianity was born. Long before Columba arrived, however, Iona was home to Druids and followers of other pagan religions. Some books call this island a "thin place," where the connection between God and humanity, the eternal and the temporal, is most apparent.

The stones on Iona have a lot to do with that feeling. On Columba's Bay, I am surrounded by stones: yellow, pink, violet, white, gray, and green, sometimes all marbled together in one rock. Some of these stones are almost three *billion* years old. Holding one of them is the closest I have ever come to imagining eternity.

Sheep bleat in the distance, and four teenagers giggle and scream as they wade in the chilly water. Up and down the rocky beach, more young people in shorts and backpacks—perhaps thirty altogether— pick up stones or sit on stones, walk on stones or throw stones into the bay. Earlier this morning, Mary Lee and I joined the weekly pilgrimage around Iona's various holy sites led by staff of the Iona Community, an ecumenical Christian organization.

The Geriatric Pilgrim

This week is the Community's annual Youth Conference, and instead of the meditative walk I imagined, Mary Lee and I have found ourselves on a gallop, the young people racing up and down hills and jumping over rocks like mountain goats, while we plod along behind, catching up at the various stations along the way, always arriving at the tag end of a prayer.

Since Laurie died fourteen years ago, I am sometimes more aware of her continued presence in my life than at other times. On the pilgrimage around Iona, I see her in these young people, the way they bounce when they run, the intensity in their eyes when they talk, their uninhibited laughter.

As always, my pleasure in my daughter's company is tempered by the loss of her physicality. Even if I can occasionally feel her touch, I cannot hold her. I cannot see her face become more interesting as it ages. Emptiness starts to burn, and I lift my eyes to the hills—to the sunlight shimmering over lichen-covered rocks.

Jennie, our student guide, calls us together. "As part of our pilgrimage," she says, raising her voice above the sound of the wind and the waves, "we take two pebbles from the beach. One we throw into the sea as a symbol of something in our lives we would like to leave behind, while the other we take back with us as a sign of a new commitment in our heart."

I watch the kids turn and race down over the rocks. I follow, not sure just what I want to leave behind, until I pick up a black-and-white-and-red stone, flat and jagged at one end. I feel once more the sharp-cornered ache that I will never—at least in this lifetime—have recompense for the loss of my child. At the water's edge, I put my index finger around the stone, and dipping my shoulder, skim the rock across the water.

Jutting out into the ocean in front of me, a rocky promontory is layered like a birthday cake, yellow turning to black, then dove gray, crowned with green-brown grass frosted with pink heather and yellow wildflowers. Splashes of yellow lichen pattern the gray rock. I've read that, in order to attach firmly to the rocks, lichens manufacture solvents capable of dissolving stone, and it occurs to me that even the ancient stones of Iona dissolve, wash to the sea, and recycle back into rock or some other organic form.

That these stones can be both eternal and transitory is something I can't fathom, but I decide it is the koan I should take back with me along with a green, heart-shaped stone I've just picked up.

I put the green heart in my pocket, turn, and clamber up the fifty or so yards of stones rising at an almost forty-five-degree angle between the water and a field. The stones shift, slide, and sink under my feet. Once I stumble and fall to my knees. Finally, I give up trying to walk straight up and begin to weave my way back and forth. When I reach the top of the final tier of stones, I turn again and look once more out over Columba's Bay. I feel Laurie nudge me with her elbow, hear her voice in my ear: "Pretty neat day I painted you, huh, Dad?"

The surf crashes, and the layers of stone shift in a chorus of clanks, thuds, clatters, pings, rattles, and taps, a Sanctus that pulls at me as Mary Lee and I trek through the boggy fields, over shimmering hills, past the cairn of Cul ri Eirinn, where Columba turned his back forever on Ireland, and across the Machair, where fairies are said to dance in the moonlight.

Being in Tanzania

WHAT KEEPS COMING BACK TO ME ABOUT OUR TRIP TO TANZANIA IS a comment our guide, Abel, made the morning he drove Mary Lee and me to the Serengeti Plain. We'd begun to see tall, red-robed people herding humpbacked cattle on the hills. He told us these were Africa's iconic Masai, the semi-nomadic tribe who live in Kenya and Tanzania, continuing their age-old customs, persisting in speaking their own language, despite both governments' instituted programs to encourage them to assimilate into the general culture.

"I like the Masai," Abel said. "They are proud just to be."

Since then, I've become aware of how hard it is for me to feel that way. Oh, I can remember when I was proud to be a varsity basketball player, proud to be a teacher, proud to be a parent and grandparent, proud to be an American. But proud just to be? The idea has always been as foreign to me as a Masai diet of blood and curdled milk. I was raised always to consider, *What will the neighbors think?* To get my worth from how others perceive me.

The problem is that I make assumptions about how others see me, which has led to a lifetime of anxiety and resentments. When I decided I no longer wanted to play basketball competitively, I was convinced people saw me as a quitter. Even after thirty years of teaching, I considered myself an abysmal failure as a human being if I had a bad class. When my daughter died from cancer, convinced people saw me as

Being in Tanzania

a poor parent who couldn't look after his child, my pride in being a father turned to shame. In Africa, I found myself embarrassed to admit to being from the United States for fear of being seen as a supporter of the policies of our then-president.

And as the morning continued, and I got used to seeing the Masai and the motorcycles and the open fires and the outdoor furniture stores beside the road on our long drive to the Serengeti, my mind reverted to playing the same old home movies it always does when it wanders. I was back in high school, changing the outcome of the state basketball championship game, winning by twenty points this time instead of losing by that much, and being carried off the court by my teammates. I argued politics with some of those same teammates whose views now differed 180 degrees from mine, destroying their feeble arguments with my brilliant sarcasm. I changed my life when I returned from this trip, eating more fruits and vegetables, giving up cheese and chocolate, losing ten pounds, growing another beard, maybe getting another tattoo—all examples of getting my identity from what I imagined would impress other people.

* * *

After lunch, we entered the Serengeti—miles and miles of lion-brown plains dotted with feathery trees under a vast sky. Abel raised the roof of his Land Cruiser. Mary Lee and I stood and began to see animals: gazelles and antelope at first, then the occasional ostrich and warthog. In the distance, a road seemed to move until we came closer and saw that it was a large herd of cape buffalo chugging across the landscape. On a large boulder, a lion gazed into the distance.

Slowly, my mind started to shift its focus, still returning between animals, however, to those old illusions and assumptions.

Until, in the late afternoon, we saw a circle of land cruisers around an acacia tree. Pulling in, I could make out a female lion sleeping on a limb. At first, peering through the same sarcastic glasses I often wear, I found the scene ridiculous—a half dozen vehicles and maybe twenty people—many with telephoto lenses the size of cannons—all for one lion trying to sleep? Then Abel gave me his binoculars and I watched the lion stretching and contracting her front legs. She swished her tail, arched her back, and moved higher into the tree. Onyx-colored eyes glanced at me dispassionately. She yawned, revealing a large tongue and sharp teeth. Behind her, the air seemed to glow golden, and great clouds towered.

When I handed the binoculars back to Abel, most of the other land cruisers had left. I realized I had no idea how long I'd been looking at the lion. Suddenly (a word that's easy for me to overuse, but in this case it really was sudden), I felt a feeling of peace, of "evenness," of lightness, followed by a sense of gratitude—Wow! I just got to see that. Thank you!

The feeling didn't last of course, but over the next week it did return and last longer: lying in our tent at night, listening to the hyenas' *r-r-r-upe, r-r-r-rip*, and the heavy breathing of what we found out later were two old male buffalo who liked to wander the grounds; the sight of over a hundred hippopotamuses wedged together like sausages in a river; herds of twenty to fifty elephants parading down to another river to drink and splash and roll in the mud; a cheetah and her two cubs prowling through the grass; seven giraffes standing silhouetted on a ridge; the strange baobab trees, a prehistoric species that predates both mankind and the splitting of the continents over two hundred million years ago, whose branches look like roots, and whose gnarled bark has been worn by wind and rain and millennia of elephants using them for scratching posts.

Now, I would say those were times I was simply *being*. That I set aside the old baggage I usually carry around and became more open, with no preconceived ideas of what I thought I needed to prove to someone else. And instead of losing the sense of who I was, I became *more* of who I was, in union with a much larger whole—not just a bunch of weird looking animals, but an energy, a spirit, if you will, running through animals, trees, grass, sky, clouds, Abel, Mary Lee, and me.

Even if you don't journey to honor a saint or to see a holy place, I think any trip can become a pilgrimage when the exterior journey triggers an interior one. I know I left some of my defensive, passive-aggressive sarcasm on the Serengeti Plain. My peripheral vision seems wider. At the same time, I care less about what others think of me. I'm still not "proud just to be," but I've become less concerned about who or what I am and more interested in *that* I am.

Food for the Journey

THE OTHER NIGHT, WHEN MARY LEE AND I WERE REMINISCING about walking St. Cuthbert's Way, we found ourselves asking each other what foods we recalled. Remember when we got off the bus in Melrose, how hungry we were and how good that ham and cheese toastie was? And that salmon in Dryburgh? Nothing was better than the lamb, though, in Jedburgh. Unless it was the scallops in Fenwick. And weren't the chips always good, no matter where we were?

Which got me thinking that food has always been part of every pilgrimage I've ever been on: Brother Bernie's blueberry pie on our first night at Emery House, run by the Brothers of the Society of St. John the Evangelist; the falafel and shawarma, figs and dates in Israel; Scottish haigis (I actually like the stuff); ploughman's lunches in England, and once for breakfast, the largest kipper I've ever seen; Irish soda bread; New Mexican tamales; just about anything on the menu in San Francisco's Chinatown; Turkish mezze platters; Nova Scotia seafood chowder.

Likewise, I often identify the stages of my life's pilgrimages by the food I remember: the smell of the bread and rolls my mother baked every Saturday morning and the taste of butter melting on hot, yeasty dough; chicken fried steak and creamed sausage over biscuits when I worked for the Forest Service in Idaho; the pizza in Orono, Maine, where I went to college; pancakes soaked in Vermont maple syrup;

baked beans and codfish cakes when I lived in Down East Maine; butterflied leg of lamb, new potatoes, and fresh corn on the cob with Mary Lee's Wellesley Fudge Cake for dessert.

I'm not sure about the future, but based on my observation of the active octogenarians and nonagenarians I know, I expect I'll eat a lot of oatmeal and ice cream.

Maybe because years of smoking have dulled my taste buds, or because I don't cook, or because it's just the way I see the world, food for me is seldom just food. For example, I think of food as romantic love. Yes, there is our traditional Valentine's night out at a four-star restaurant, but thirty-six years ago, after Mary Lee and I stood on the rocks of Casco Bay with an Episcopal priest who blessed our civil marriage, the three of us went to the local pizza place, which is still where Mary Lee and I go on our anniversary.

When I had basketball practice in high school, my mother made the rest of the family wait to eat dinner until I got home. I really didn't care if they waited for me, and I think my father was pissed, but since then, I've read that one of the marks of successful, well-adjusted young people is that they eat dinner with their families—something that happens less and less in these days of individual TVs, computers, sports practices, and erratic work schedules. Food, then, helps bond the family unit.

Don't most family celebrations revolve around food? Thanksgiving is the big bash for us. Ever since Mary Lee and I lived in a small apartment with next to no money, beginning our lives all over again at the age of forty, we hosted our families—adults sitting on couches with TV trays, children on the stairs, so that grandparents could sit at our tiny dining room table. (Not that we had a dining room.) We felt it important to make both sides of our family know they were part of our new lives. Now, as the oldest members of our family, we host not only Thanksgiving, but also often Christmas, Easter, and birthdays, as a way to stay connected to the next generations.

Food is friendship. Still another activity I missed because of the pandemic was that after my weekly men's group meeting at our church, most of us used to go for coffee at a local bakery, where I'd have some kind of muffin, scone, or coffee cake, savoring the calories and the conversation. Even now, every month or so, I join the ROMEOs (Retired Old Men Eating Out), from the high school class of 1961 for lunch at an area restaurant with outdoor seating. Sometimes, we search out new places for German or Indian or Japanese food; other times we return to old standbys for fish & chips, burgers, and fried clams. But the kind and quality of the food is not the reason we're often the first customers to arrive and some of the last to leave.

When my non-churchgoing friends ask me why I go to church every week and several times a day when I'm on retreat, I say I go to be fed. I've never known what happens to that wafer and wine on Sunday, but I'll take it. And, up until COVID, I did. And look forward to doing so again.

During a brief flirtation with Buddhism, I attended six-hour sesshins that, in addition to silent meditation, included walking meditation, talking meditation, and eating meditation. At the end of the day, we were served tea and a cookie. That cookie was the best-tasting cookie I'd ever eaten. A year or so later, after I'd decided I was a Christian and had stopped going to these sesshins, I discovered those same cookies in the grocery store. I brought them home and made a cup of tea. At my kitchen table, away from the Zen community that had fed me, those same cookies tasted like cardboard.

So maybe the lesson here—for me at least—is that the meals I remember have less to do with food and more to do with the companions who've been with me when I've eaten that food (the word "companion" literally means "with bread"), and if I am to continue to live, not just exist, I need to be nourished by more than oatmeal and ice cream.

Back Story

FOR THE LAST FIFTY YEARS, BACK PAIN HAS BEEN A CONSTANT IN MY life—through two marriages, six jobs, retirement, and the deaths of my parents, a daughter, and many friends. I've had a back fusion that laid me up for four months (and accomplished nothing), plus visits to chiropractors, orthopedists, and acupuncturists costing me thousands of dollars (ditto).

It was my acupuncturist, however, who suggested a book to me on the psychology of back pain. I didn't buy the author's theory that anger is the cause of all back pain, but I did start a pilgrimage of sorts through my internal landscape of other half-buried emotions to see what I might unearth.

Linear person that I am, I went back (no pun intended) to the beginning.

* * *

In early March, 1968, I received my draft notice to report for an Army physical in April. I shouldn't have been surprised. The previous year, the number of US troops stationed in Vietnam had risen to half a million, and there were calls for even more troops. The previous summer, I'd been notified that my military deferment for being married and for being a teacher had ended.

The Geriatric Pilgrim

Still, I'd ignored my new 1-A draft card. I was at the University of Vermont, entering my second semester as a graduate assistant in English, married, living comfortably in an apartment maybe a half mile from the UVM campus. Academia had opened a wonderful new world for me, an inner world of the mind, removed from outside influences (like a war), and I was focused on getting into a PhD program and becoming a college English professor.

Then came the draft notice. I didn't know what to do. One of my teaching-assistant colleagues told me he had contacts in Montreal, just ninety-six miles away, should I want to defect. I thought about it, but realized I was no conscientious objector; I just thought the war was stupid.

My wife, whose cousin had just shipped out to Vietnam, seemed resigned to my going, saying she would return to live with her parents in Maine and wait for me. (Thirty-five years after our divorce, I wonder if she wasn't secretly looking forward to going back to Maine and being closer to her parents.)

Well, I decided if I have to go, I'll do it on my terms: I'll enlist in the Navy, and since, if I do that, I'll have to serve four years, I might as well become an officer. Which, as I write this, doesn't make any sense, since, given my age of twenty-five and my academic background, I doubt I'd have seen combat, and my Army tour of duty would have been only two years. Still, two days after receiving my draft notice, I went down to the Navy recruiting office and signed up for officer's candidate school. Which meant taking the Navy's physical examination, which meant going to the Springfield, Massachusetts, Armory the following weekend.

I recall that most men taking the physical were younger than I, of various ethnicities, dressed in everything from ripped jeans to hippie tie-dyes to one guy in a suit and tie. Hair length was even more varied. We were given lockers and told to strip to our underwear. I don't remember all the various preliminary tests except for being so nervous I couldn't pee in the cup. But I must have eventually because I wound up in a sort of gymnasium in my boxers. A deep voice told us to drop our shorts and lean forward while some guys in uniforms went behind us shining flashlights up our asses.

Then, the voice told us to bend over and touch our toes. In the row in front of me was a guy in a back brace. He raised his hand, and the officer motioned for him to get out of line. He yelled, "Okay, anyone who can't touch his toes because of a back problem, fall in over here!"

For the previous two weeks, I had thought and thought of ways to deal with my draft notice and had only become more and more confused. Now, without thinking, I followed the guy with the back brace to a room on the edge of the floor. Only after I was walking behind him did I realize what I was about to do and remember why I was going to do it.

When I was sixteen, I'd hurt my back in a high school physical education class. My mother drove me to the hospital for x-rays. A young man—probably some kind of intern or maybe a technician—came out to say that I'd broken my back. Of course, I was upset. The guy left, but then a few minutes later a doctor entered. "No," he said, "you haven't broken your back, just bruised it. But," he continued, "you have a deformity in your lower back that looks like it could be a break." He called it Scheuermann's Disease, which I've since found is a curvature in the middle of the back caused by a period of accelerated growth (two years earlier, I'd grown four inches in a year). My Scheuermann's was especially pronounced, with two vertebrae jutting noticeably from my spine.

"Remember," said the doctor, "if you're ever in an automobile accident, it will look like you have a broken back."

After the bruising went away, I forgot all about Scheuermann and his disease. I played basketball and fought forest fires and did just about any physical activity I wanted to with no pain whatsoever. Nine years later, however, walking behind this guy in a back brace, it all came back to me, so when I sat down in that room by this desk with another military type, I was ready. Did I have a history of back problems? Yes, ever since I was sixteen. Did it keep me from physical activity? Yes. (There was one exercise on the obstacle course that we had when I was in the forest service that I thought I couldn't do because I couldn't bend all the way back and touch my head to the ground behind me. Of course, few other guys could do that one, either.) Was I experiencing pain right now? Yes. (And as I sat there, my lower back really did hurt.) Okay, son, come back here next week and we'll take some x-rays.

A month after those x-rays, I received notice that my military status had changed from 1-A to 1-Y, which meant qualified only in time of national emergency.

I was home free.

* * *

Except it's been since that time that I've had back problems.

So, I wonder, is the pain due to guilt? Recently, at the men's group I belong to, several Vietnam vets were reminiscing, and I came home with my back throbbing. Somewhere, I'd heard the term "survivor guilt." Going to my trusted Wikipedia, I read, "Survivor guilt…occurs when a person believes they have done something wrong by surviving a traumatic or tragic event when others did not, often feeling self-guilt."

Could be. The Vietnam war killed two of my classmates in combat, caused a friend to suffer years of depression, another friend to become an alcoholic, and a third to die from cancer caused by the defoliant Agent Orange.

In many cases of survivor guilt, the article goes on to say, survivors spend a lifetime compensating for the guilt of having survived by doing good things. That military physical certainly changed my goals and values. I went home to the University of Vermont less interested in academics and more interested in helping others, and I can honestly say that I did more good in the next two years than I would have sitting at a desk typing Army reports or standing on the bridge of a destroyer. Instead of becoming a college professor, I returned to teaching high school students from all backgrounds, some of whom I've stayed in contact with for over forty years. I became an active member of a church community, working with youth groups and with the homeless.

All of which I started telling my back.

Did it help? Has the pain gone away?

Yes and no. The pain is still there, but I find simply by my being aware of the guilt that might be causing it (emphasis on *might*, as I could be psychobabbling), my back pain has diminished to back discomfort, discomfort I accept because of a choice I once made and would make again.

The Stories We Carry

All the books and articles on pilgrimage I've read stress the importance of traveling light. I agree, but there are also things I've had to carry with me. One such thing is the fragment of a children's story I wrote about my daughter and her best friend, Sharon, who lived next door to us almost fifty years ago.

The girls were both about five at the time, both were the same size, and both wore their hair short with straight bangs across their foreheads. But while Laurie was fair-skinned and blond, Sharon was dark-complexioned, with the blackest hair I think I've ever seen. Cuddled together on the patio settee, they looked like Yin and Yang.

My story told of Melilia and Gotha, two little girls, one with blond hair and one with black hair, and began just after some catastrophe had befallen the world—I can't remember now if it was a nuclear war, or if the earth had been bombarded by asteroids, or if creatures from outer space were stealing children for slaves. Anyway, Melilia and Gotha journey along the rockbound coast of Maine, following the instructions of Melilia's dying parents, who have told her if she can get to the Celestial Islands off the coast, she will find peace and safety. As Melilia and Gotha struggle over the rocky bluffs, they are set upon by sidehill badgers, so named because the legs on one side of their bodies are longer than those on the other side, which allow them to move quickly around the piles of rocks, the males moving clockwise and the females counterclockwise. The sidehill badgers are odious and ferocious creatures, and Melilia and Gotha might have been captured and eaten had it not been for a pipe-smoking sea turtle (I smoked a pipe in those days) who comes out of the ocean to drive the badgers back to their caves.

I never got any further in the narrative and probably would have forgotten all about the story, except ten years later, I read that Sharon, whose family had moved away earlier, had been murdered, stabbed in the back some fifteen times. Police arrested a thirty-one-year-old patient at the Augusta Mental Health Institute who, over the last ten years, had attacked three different women with knives, but who, for some reason, had been given court-authorized permission to leave the AMHI campus unsupervised for several hours a day.

Three years later, a routine biopsy of a cyst on the back of Laurie's head revealed a malignant tumor at the base of her brain.

* * *

After Laurie died, my story of two innocent girls beset upon by catastrophe was like a great weight. Why couldn't Laurie's mother and I have been the ones to die like they do in the story, instead of our daughter and her friend? Why couldn't I protect them the way my avatar, the turtle, did? And a celestial home of peace and safety? Hah! All I could see was a world of nastiness and death.

So I tried to throw the story away. I spent a lot of time in my den, drinking myself into forgetfulness. I read existential philosophy, especially Albert Camus's *Myth of Sisyphus*, in which the author sees Sisyphus—condemned by the gods to forever roll a rock to the top of a mountain, from where the stone falls back because of its own weight—as representing how humanity tries to impose meaning on a meaningless world, a condition the author labels "absurd." Made sense to me. To look for any meaning in Laurie's cancer and Sharon's murder was,

The Geriatric Pilgrim

I decided, absurd. Their deaths were statistical accidents, like being struck by lightning. The story of Melilia and Gotha was merely that: a story. *Get rid of it*, I told myself. *Otherwise, it will continue to roll back on you, like Sisyphus's stone.*

Except I couldn't, and it didn't. Although I certainly felt for a long time that I was pushing the same rock up the same mountain, gradually I became aware that I was on a journey similar to Mililia and Gotha's—picking my way along a rocky coastline of shame, sorrow, and despair, beset upon by any number of nasty creatures (many of my own making), but saved by an equal number of protectors—loved ones, counselors, spiritual mentors—who appeared out of an ocean of compassion when I most needed them.

Which makes me realize—perhaps for the first time—that I've always envisioned some kind of ocean bay beside Mililia and Gotha on their travels, but never thought about it because I've always taken oceans for granted. Still, the sea has always been for me a source of healing, of cleansing. I grew up in a coastal community in Maine. I first learned to swim in Casco Bay. After living in Vermont for four years, I moved back to Maine because I missed the ocean. When I was teaching, I almost always took the long way home from work so I could drive by water. Whenever I've made pilgrimages, I've often sought out places close to the sea.

I recall an August 9th, on what would have been Laurie's forty-sixth birthday, when Mary Lee, my sister, Jaye, and I took a cruise around Casco Bay: a mini-pilgrimage, in homage to the young woman we loved. For the first time in years, we cruised by islands we'd all visited years before, often with Laurie. It was a great day. Jaye remembered taking Laurie with her digging clams off Little John's Island, the two of them plastered with mud and seaweed. Mary Lee remembered the summer of Laurie's chemotherapy, when we took her and her stepbrothers on a whale watch, and instead of Laurie, it was Mary Lee who got seasick. I recalled coming through the channel between Long Island and Chebeague Island with Laurie and Mary Lee, a wave catching our little sixteen-foot boat and throwing it just inches from a humongous ledge.

I came home feeling healed—saved, if you will.

*　*　*

Even on pilgrimage, you can't leave the past behind. But I've found that what a pilgrimage can do is redeem the past—give it back to you, transformed, enfolded. George Fox, founder of the Society of Friends, or Quakers, wrote in 1647:

> *I saw that there was an ocean of darkness and death, but an infinite ocean of light and love, that flowed over the ocean of darkness. In that, I also saw the infinite love of God....*

At one point on our cruise, the captain called our attention to two dolphins playing in the channel between our boat and an island. As I watched them roll and leap and plunge, it seemed to me that I could see Melilia and Gotha on their backs, laughing and singing, on their way to the Celestial Islands.

Our Embedded Remains

OF COURSE, NOT EVERY TRIP NEEDS TO BE A PILGRIMAGE.

I know, I know. Given the title of this book and the pilgrimages and retreats I'm describing, you'd think the only worthwhile journeys I've ever made have involved intense planning, a degree of discomfort, and an even greater degree of "spirituality."

But a few years ago, Mary Lee and I had a wonderful trip to Turkey. Our purpose was to visit friends and to escape a Maine winter that had extended, as it often does, into April. For a week, we were chauffeured around and fed royally by Lynne and Finlay, who, after teaching in Istanbul for ten years, had bought a home in Selcuk (as in "sell-chuck") in the western part of the country. I hadn't prepared for the trip and knew next to nothing about Turkey except that the apostle Paul, one of Christianity's heroes, spent a lot of time there.

I had no idea that the ancient city of Ephesus, where Paul lived for a while and for whom he may have written one of his Epistles, is part of Selcuk. Nor did I know that Selcuk is also the site of the Temple of Artemis, one of the Seven Wonders of the Ancient World; the Basilica of St. John, built on the tomb of John the Beloved Disciple and author (perhaps) of the Bible's Book of Revelation; the home of the Virgin Mary, where Jesus's mother is thought by pilgrims to have spent her last days; and Isa Bey Mosque, which dates from the fourteenth century.

And perhaps because I didn't come to Turkey as a pilgrim, or perhaps because the hordes of tourists—a lot of Asians, Germans, and Australians—reminded me of the tourists in Old Orchard and Bar Harbor in Maine, none of these places ever felt particularly holy to me.

What I did feel was a palpable sense of history. For centuries, Turkey has resided at the crossroads between Eastern and Western cultures. Part of Istanbul is in Europe and part of the city is in Asia. Turkey is where Noah's ark is supposed to have come to ground after the flood. The Grand Fortress of Selcuk rests on the site of castles going back to before 5000 BCE. Before becoming a republic in 1923, the country was, at various times, part of Greek, Roman, Christian, and Islamic empires.

And I'm not exaggerating when I say this history is palpable; visitors can see and touch it. Turkey's historic civilizations are literally embedded in one another, stone next to stone, sometimes in strange ways—carved marble cornices in the middle of granite walls, for example.

This embedded history is clearly evident in Selcuk. You find very little left of the Temple of Artemis, once known throughout the ancient world for its mix of classic Greek and Near Eastern design, because after its final destruction in 262 CE, its marble stones were used in construction of later buildings, including the Basilica of St. John. And when the Basilica became unusable after a fourteenth-century earthquake, some of its stones, along with stones from the Temple of Artemis were used to build Isa Bey Mosque in 1375.

* * *

Even on vacation, you can never entirely escape your own history. Seeing and touching the stones that make up Selcuk's past, I couldn't help wondering if, just as Turkey's civilizations were built using the remains of previous cultures, who I am today isn't built of some of the destroyed remains of previous selves I've reassembled.

Anyone reading this who's lost a child understands how your entire world—past, present, and future—is destroyed. All your old landmarks become rubble, and you have no point of reference, nothing to guide you. You wander lost and fearful.

But maybe one of the ways we grieving parents survive is by embedding parts of our old, destroyed selves into transformed ones, possibly becoming stronger in the process.

I was raised in the Christian tradition. If I could draw pictures of my early faith, they would resemble a child's book of an idealized 1950s small town, filled with quaint Andy Griffin meets Ozzie and Harriet characters. God was, like my pastor and next-door neighbor, Scotty Campbell, a nice guy who winked and always seemed to be around, even when your parents were busy. As I grew older, I replaced those images with a Sierra Club calendar of majestic, forest-covered mountains glowing in a brilliant sunrise, filled with possibility. When I met Mary Lee, I added more images to include her, the two of us being guided along bucolic trails by a creative, loving Presence.

And then I learned that this God could create not only purple mountains' majesty but cancer cells. At first, God disappeared, then reappeared as the Great Sadist, inflicting pain on innocent children. Eventually, God became the Great Opponent, with whom I, like the Biblical Jacob, wrestled until I finally surrendered to what I now think of as the Great Mystery of Grace.

Today, I realize that, should I try to blueprint my faith, it would look a lot like some of the buildings Mary Lee and I saw in Turkey, with images of God as caretaker, God as creator, God as opponent, God as mystery, God as lover, embedded—along with sorrow and joy, doubt and faith, shame and compassion, grief and hope—into a single edifice: God of My Not Understanding.

Sort of the way, come to think of it, a pilgrimage can sometimes become embedded in a vacation.

We Pilgrims

YOU'RE LOOKING AT A PHOTOGRAPH FROM ONE OF MY HIGH SCHOOL reunions. The class of 1961 is standing on a beach in front of Sebago Lake, Maine under storm-driven clouds that will eventually drive us inside the pavilion and cancel our boat ride. Probably because of my interest in pilgrimages, I look at the photograph and see all of us now as pilgrims, on reunion every five years or so to catch up on where our journeys have taken us.

Along the way, most of us have gained weight. Men have gone gray, white, or bald. Some of the women are gray haired and buxom, while others color their hair and show that sinewy look that comes from

The Geriatric Pilgrim

regular aerobic exercise. Most of the class is smiling. Several of us in the front row don't know what to do with our hands, so we cross them in front of ourselves, like those paintings of Adam and Eve after they learn about sin and realize they're naked.

Reunions are a unique combination of past and present. One minute four of us guys rhapsodize about drag racing over the Cousins Island Bridge, while the next minute we compare the fiber contents in our breakfast cereals. Gazing into the picture, I can hear Doug's *haw-haw-haw* booming over the sand the same way it used to echo in the gym when we called him "Spider." Some of us who used to work in Bornheimer's Market Garden are chuckling about how many beet greens we'd be able to cut these days. My old jazz band, The Ivy Leaguers, remembers our appearance on Channel 6's *Youth Cavalcade*.

We began our respective pilgrimages by crossing the threshold of the familiar and going separate but parallel ways. At some point, we all wore tie-dyes and long hair, went to Vietnam, saw Nixon's name on the ballot and waited in gas lines. We've listened to Elvis and Little Richard, Dylan and Baez, the Beatles and the Stones; we've given up cigarettes and taken up bottled water, personal computers, and cell phones.

Like all pilgrims, we've had to relinquish our grasp on certainty and control. We've been to one degree or another broken. Half of us—the national average—are divorced. Most of us have lost our parents, some have lost brothers or sisters, and several of us have lost children.

And then there's our own decay. We try to make fun of our creaky backs and artificial hips and knees and arthritic shoulders, the hearing aids and pacemakers, but cancer and COPD and CHF are not laughing matters. Over 25 percent of our class has died, mostly to cancer and heart failure. I recall Marty, who'd already died from cancer of the esophagus when this picture was taken, and Tom who died from lung cancer shortly afterward. I hear Marty and me singing "Palisades Park" in his uncle's Ford as we peel out of the Scarborough A&W Drive-In; I watch Tom and me playing pool at the Pine Tree Billiards Center—"The Tree"—in Portland.

We Pilgrims

A pilgrimage requires a degree of discomfort, even sacrifice. At least half of the men standing on this beach in front of Sebago Lake served in the military. Most of us—men and women—have put in long hours working to support our families. A few of us are still working. We've gotten out of bed in the middle of the night to look after our sick children, taken aging parents into our homes, sat in the hospital with ailing parents, siblings, and children.

But in the process of being broken, we've received gifts far greater than we ever could have imagined in 1961: children and grandchildren, the knowledge that we have been loved, the solace of memories, the joy of lasting friendships.

Of course, the fact that we came from a small graduating class in a little Maine town may explain why so many aspects of our journeys look the same. We had no minorities, no "one-percenters," no refugees, nobody who was not a US citizen, and, as far as I know, nobody for whom English wasn't a first language. Even our differences reflect a common background. Some of us look back with nostalgia at the way we lived sixty years ago. It's a rare month that I don't receive an email or Facebook litany of all the ways our lives were better than those of today's kids: we worked harder, we were better disciplined, we were healthier, smarter, better looking, and more respectful. Our pleasures were simpler, our food was better, and our music was cooler.

Others of us remember the narrow-minded small-town provincialism, the lack of opportunities for women, prejudice against gays ("homos," we called them), French Canadians, Jews, the closet alcoholism and sexual abuse, the lack of education for those of us with learning disabilities, the jock culture, and teacher brutality.

There are those of us who want to keep things the way we remember them being when we grew up, and those of us who want to eliminate those prejudices and provide more opportunities. At no time is this more evident than during election years. And because of the acerbic nature of recent campaigns, it's almost impossible to avoid the rhetoric that masquerades as discussion. I cringe every time one of my classmates posts something espousing his or her political stance, no matter the position. (Okay, okay. I cringe more when it's a view counter to mine, and suppress the urge to hit the "Like" icon when I see something that says what I've been thinking.)

But as the philosopher said, this, too, shall pass. We in the class of '61 are tied together in deep and special ways. We know things about each other that no one, not even our parents or our spouses or partners, let alone our children, know: sneaking into the Yarmouth Drive-In movie theater by hiding in the trunk of Scott's car, Craig bouncing a cue ball through the window of George Soule's pool room, Jerry letting the tarantula out of the jar in Mr. List's biology class. We share not only a history, but also a private language ("Fire up!" "Walk on it one time!")

And our largely homogeneous class also walks the larger human pilgrimage. Although we have different ideas of where our journey leads and what it means, we're all hoping to find our way to a better place. And, as with all pilgrims, no matter where we've gone, no matter to whom we've paid homage, no matter what gifts we've received on our journey, we are all eventually called home.

Some are already there, waiting to welcome the rest of us.

A Pilgrim's Journal: August 9, 2003

Yarmouth, Maine

I LOOK AT THE FADED AND FOLDED WHITE LINED PAPER, AT LAURIE'S tiny, circular handwriting: "This sandwich would win the approval of Henri Matisse, and fans of rainbows as well." Suddenly I hear her in the kitchen, opening the refrigerator, taking out containers, opening the vegetable tray. Rustle of cellophane, clink of glass, thud of food hitting the counter.

"Dad, where's the vinegar?"

I realize she's never been in this house. "In the bottom cupboard, behind the second door over from the fridge. Do you want some help?"

"Nope, I'm fine."

I know she's wearing an oversized tee shirt she's tie-dyed, one like she did for me. I hear her singing to herself, probably something by Suzanne Vega, or Tracy Chapman: "Don't you know they're talkin' 'bout a revolution. It sounds like a whisper."

"Peacenik!" I yell.

"Flower power lives!" she yells back. "Where's the red onion?"

"Under the cupboard on the counter by the window. In that basket."

I hear chopping sounds, then the rasp of vegetables against a grater. I jump at the whirring and rattling of our blender, then jump again when Laurie cries, "Yikes!" and the blender stops

I stand. "What's wrong?"

"Nothing." She laughs. "The top came off the blender. I've just got this dressing all over the counter and all over me. I'll clean it up."

I smile and sit back down at my desk. "No problem. But this seems like a lot of work for a sandwich."

"Da-a-ad! This just isn't any sandwich. It's a work of art."

And for a minute, I see her in the doorway, dressed as I imagined, blue cheese sauce splattered on her arms and a dab of it on her nose. She looks at me, one eyebrow raised, her forehead furrowed in what I think of as a combination of amusement, satisfaction, and frustration. My daughter, the artist. Whether she's painting a landscape, playing the piano, embroidering, woodburning, or cooking, she throws herself into it.

And then I see the bright red bandanna around her head, the one she wore during the chemotherapy treatments, and my vision of my daughter fades. I'm staring at her last self-portrait, at her sad eyes gazing wistfully out through a window at the world. In the kitchen, Mary Lee is pouring herself a cup of coffee.

Today would have been Laurie's thirty-third birthday, and my only child has been dead almost fifteen years. It's a bittersweet day, a sandwich of emotions: a layer of sorrow, a layer of rage. Chop up some shame, some guilt, and some regret. Mix in some "if onlys," and a few "what ifs." Season that mixture for a while, let the sharpness mellow. Top it with a generous mixture of happy memories, ongoing love, and the knowledge that you helped create someone beautiful and loving and courageous beyond measure, someone who touched all who knew her, inspired many, made a difference for the better in this world—all by the age of eighteen.

I'm still not sure how to celebrate her birthday, figure out how to hold both the knowledge that she is gone with the awareness that she's always with me. Today, I will buy some flowers and take them to her memorial stone in our family cemetery. Laurie's stepmother and I will walk along the ocean, not on some sandy beach crowded with oiled brown bodies and the smell of grease, but a rocky shore where waves hiss and crash on weathered stones and the seaweed smells of damp musk, and I can feel the wind in my face, drying my tears as I pray: "Watch over Thy Child, O Lord, as her days increase; bless and guide her wherever she may be...."

When we come home, I will follow the recipe for blue cheese sandwiches that Laurie copied for us from the *Moosewood Cookbook* a year or so before she died. Ordinarily, I hate to cook, but for this one time of the year I will prepare a meal instead of simply opening a can of soup or a package of risotto. I'll shred and chop and sauté and be the one covered in blue cheese sauce. I'll skin my knuckles on the grater.

But hey, as Laurie says, this is not just any sandwich.

(Note: This essay appeared in the magazine *Alimentum: The Literature of Food*.)

Stan

Several years ago, when I was signing copies of my novel *Requiem in Stones* at a book fair, I got talking to this guy who said he'd grown up in in Yarmouth, Maine, some hundred miles to the south.

"Hey, I did, too!" I said.

"I know. Your sister emailed me that you'd be here. My name is John Haskell."

Well, I hadn't seen John for at least fifty years. As we chatted, I told him at one point how much I'd always admired his father, and I spent much of my drive home thinking about all the ways John's father, Stan, kept reappearing in my life—times that marked important turns in this loopy, looping pilgrimage I've been on.

When I was growing up in Yarmouth in the 1950s, Stan was manager of the local bank, a respected figure in what was then a small rural town instead of today's suburbia by the sea. He and his wife Ethel were friends of my parents. Their three children corresponded roughly in age with my brother, sister, and me, and I recall spending time at their farm by the railroad tracks in North Yarmouth, waving at engineers and conductors on the trains rolling past, picking blueberries, and jumping from the barn loft into what seemed like mountains of hay.

One day—I'd guess I was maybe eight or nine years old—some of my friends and I were playing cowboys, and we decided we'd rob the bank. We raced down the street and up the steps of the granite-gray building, pulled bandannas over our faces, drew our cap pistols, and pushed open the doors, yelling, "Stick 'em up! This is a hold-up!"

Stan never missed a beat. He threw up his hands. "Don't shoot!" he cried. "Here's the dough." And he gave us each a penny.

When I was in high school, Stan shocked everyone by selling his historic eighteenth-century farmhouse, resigning from his job, and moving his wife and three children to Bangor, where he began attending classes at Bangor Theological Seminary and the University of Maine at Orono. Most people in town agreed he was crazy. "Don't know how he can feed his family doing that," snorted my barber. Even my parents thought forty a little late to become a student.

I don't know how Stan and his family ate, but I do know that during my senior year at UMO, who should wind up sitting next to me in an education class but Stan, completing his eight years of training for the ministry. I wasn't interested in religion then and only thought about God as an intellectual jigsaw puzzle to work on when I had time to kill, but Stan was easy to talk to—he seemed so much younger than my parents—and I remained impressed at how he had thrown aside a steady job and a respected position in town to become a minister.

Four years later, fresh out of grad school, I began teaching at a new consolidated high school serving four towns on the coast of Maine. In need of a summer job, I became a seasonal policeman, gesturing with my hand for tourists to slow down as they drove through one of those towns. Maybe a week or so into the job, I tapped the air and this car screeched to a halt. Who should get out of the car but Stan, now minister of the local Congregational church. Even though I spent my Sundays walking the woods instead of sitting in church, I enjoyed getting together with Stan that first year and learning about the school district—how difficult it had been for its individual communities to give up their basketball rivalries and send their kids to one school.

One day when I told him how upset I was that some students had egged my house on Halloween, he told me of his own struggles to become accepted by his parishioners and urged me to stay with it. I wound up staying at that school for sixteen years.

As time went by, Stan became pastor aboard the Maine Seacoast Mission's *Sunbeam*, "God's Tugboat," serving the islands of Penobscot Bay. I became a father. Although my wife and I hadn't set foot in a church since our marriage, I decided I wanted our daughter Laurie baptized, so I contacted Stan. He suggested I sit down and write what I wanted him to say.

What? Wasn't there a service he was supposed to follow?

Yes, but maybe the reason I wasn't going to church, he said, was because the language of the church no longer spoke to me. What did I want from God? Why did I feel the need to have my child baptized?

Good questions, ones I couldn't answer, except that the more I thought about it, the more I wanted, even needed, to have Laurie baptized. At some level, I also realized I needed God. Maybe, I decided, I should start attending church to find out why.

I remember one more conversation with Stan. By then, I was active in the church, advising a youth group, and I ran into Stan at a state gathering. I asked how he was doing. He was tired, he said, and he looked it—thinner, stooped, black circles under his eyes. I knew he was the age of my parents. My father had recently died of cancer. "Stan, you need to slow down," I said.

"But there's so much more God wants me to do."

That was the last time I saw him. The tectonic plates of my life collided soon afterward—divorce, remarriage, followed by my daughter's cancer diagnosis and her death. When Stan himself died less than a year after my daughter, I was too caught up in my own grief to give his passing much attention.

The older I get, the more I look back over my life, however, it seems appropriate to recall with gratitude the ways Stan acted as a kind of Gandalf figure for me, popping up at opportune times to serve as mentor and guide.

Stan

He was one of the kindest men I ever met, and in the *True* Magazine culture of the '50s, a compassionate man was unusual, even countercultural. He respected the dignity of even eight-year-old bank robbers. And speaking of countercultural, before I ever heard of Jack Kerouac and the Beat Generation and "Question Authority" bumper stickers, it was Stan who taught my adolescent self to question the collective wisdom of a parochial, conservative Maine town that labeled a forty-year man "crazy" to want to become minister.

Stan was an inspiration to me in my forties, when I realized I had to change my own life dramatically, feeling, as he had, called by a power greater than myself, even though I knew I was bringing upheaval to my family. In my fifties, when I decided to take early retirement from teaching, and in my sixties, when I became a student again, I thought again of Stan, twenty years older than the rest of us, sitting in a classroom at the University of Maine.

Stan was the first clergyperson I'd ever heard be critical of the church and its practices, while at the same time, maintaining a rock-solid faith in God. He railed against what he called "totem pole communities," where people venerate their buildings instead of God. He felt the church should be out in the community, educating the poor on how to get the most from their welfare checks. Rather than preaching to his congregations about God, he preferred engaging them in discussions about God. For Stan, Jesus was to be followed, not worshipped.

And now, older than Stan when he died, tempted to put my feet up and focus what's left of my energy on getting a larger-screen TV or trading up for a newer, bigger car, I hear Stan's voice: "But there's so much more God wants me to do."

He remains a yardstick by which I continue to measure my growth, from small-town cowboy to geriatric pilgrim.

The Annual Pilgrimage

In the 1950s and '60s, high school basketball was the king of Maine sports. Communities rallied around their teams, and the twice-weekly games were the social events of the season. Fights broke out, tires were slashed, romances began and ended before, during, and after the games.

One of the highlights, not only of the winter, but of the year, were the high school basketball tournaments. Not only did schools shut down for the week, businesses closed. Some townspeople took their vacations in February, not to fly to Florida but to drive to Lewiston, eat at Stickino's Restaurant, and watch the Western Maine Basketball Tournament at the Memorial Armory.

I first heard the call to become part of what I now think of as the annual pilgrimage to Lewiston in the eighth grade when I began playing basketball. By the following year, while I might have gone to church on Sunday and listened to my pastor and next-door neighbor, Scotty Campbell, tell us about a loving God, my real worship service was in my backyard, shooting my new yellow Voit basketball into the hoop my father had put up over the garage door. My scriptures were the sports pages of the *Portland Press Herald* and the *Portland Evening Express*, my icons the pictures I cut from *Sport* magazine: Hot Rod Hundley, Bob Cousy, Bill Russell.

The Annual Pilgrimage

The twenty-six-mile drive from Yarmouth to Lewiston took us small-town kids into another world: a city of bright lights and dark allies, where everyone, it seemed, spoke French, and tall spires of stone churches loomed against the horizon. The cavernous Memorial Armory inspired an even greater feeling of awe.

But as with any good pilgrimage, it was the journey itself that was as important as the destination. Riding on the team bus, I learned about sex (even though at least half the information was wrong), what makes a good joke, and any number of songs. I learned how to hold my own swapping insults—what we called "cutting"—and I made friendships that continue to this day.

The first time I walked into the armory, I realized at some level I'd crossed the threshold into what today I call liminal space—out of ordinary time, neither past nor present nor future. The smell of smoke, sweat, and popcorn was like incense to my nostrils. My ordinary life—my family, my interests in music and reading, even my fantasies about girls—dissolved, and I was completely in the moment, focused only on the other team, the basketball, the basket.

In those days, the Western Maine Basketball Tournament consisted of eight teams each from small, medium, and large schools. The teams with the best win/loss records played those with lesser records, with the winner going on to play other winners until there was only one winner left: the Western Maine Class S, M, and L Champions, who would then face the Eastern Maine Champions in the even bigger cities of Portland or Bangor. Every game was a thirty-two-minute morality play, complete with heroes—our guys—and villains—their guys. There were always upsets, increasing the drama. And, of course, there were more losing teams than winning ones: one of life's great lessons.

Pilgrimage is often about dealing with disappointment, learning from mistakes. It's interesting to me that during the four years I played basketball for North Yarmouth Academy, the town's high school at the time, our team lost no more than maybe a dozen games, and

The Geriatric Pilgrim

yet I remember the losses far more than the victories. For three years, NYA won its first tournament games and then met Freeport in the Western Maine Finals, where we lost every time. During my senior year, we finally beat Freeport, as well as all the other teams we faced in the Western Maine Tournament, besting Cape Elizabeth to win the Class L Championship. I remember little about any of those games. What I do remember vividly, over sixty years later, is our loss to Orono in the State Championship. I can tell you the score—74–52—as well as where I scored each of my ten points—one long jump shot to start the game, two foul-line jump shots, one put back off a rebound, and two foul shots.

Pilgrimage, however, is also about beginning again. For me, the next basketball season started the day after the tournament ended. I estimate that during my four years in high school, I had a basketball in my hand 350 days a year. I was always looking ahead to the next year. Playing basketball gave my life meaning and purpose. It gave me hope.

One reason I had such a hard time adjusting to college was that, once I stopped playing organized basketball, I no longer had the next season to look forward to, nothing to work toward. This turned out to be a great lesson, one I've needed and still need more than ever these days: for serenity, I have to have a goal—some kind of basket, if you will—to shoot for.

As a teacher, I continued to attend the high school tournaments as a spectator, watching the game change, observing some of my former opponents in the crowds or refereeing the games. And I still watch the occasional tournament game on Maine's Public Television channel.

I watch as some people go to church occasionally, as reminders of how the experiences of my youth have molded me. For example, there was always a spiritual component to basketball for me. Those many hours I spent shooting my yellow ball into the makeshift hoop—the sense of first extending and then leaving myself, as if the ball were part of me, so that releasing the ball toward the basket was like soaring into the air, leaving the secular world behind—I see now as precursor to years of meditation.

The Annual Pilgrimage

And in the months after Laurie's death, I found myself thinking of Mr. Beal, my first basketball coach, and the way he had driven me. I heard his voice sometimes in the morning, "Come on, Wile, move it!" and I began to think of my grief as a basketball opponent, one I needed to work as hard to defeat as I had had to work to beat Freeport.

Except for some rural parts of the state, basketball is no longer king of Maine sports. Hockey, football, soccer, lacrosse—both men's and women's teams—all draw big crowds. A good thing, I think. (People who talk about the good old days seem to forget how few opportunities there were then for women to participate in much of anything except cheerleading.)

The Lewiston Armory is no longer the site for high school tournaments, but it is still hosts recreation programs, gun shows, the Androscoggin Falls Angels Roller Derby League, and, once a year, large numbers of the Somalis now residing in Lewiston who gather to celebrate Eid al-Fitr, the end of Ramadan.

Nice to see that the Amory remains a destination for pilgrims.

Work as Pilgrimage

A FRIEND WHO KNOWS I WRITE ABOUT PILGRIMAGE HAS GIVEN ME A book, *Crossing the Unknown Sea: Work as a Pilgrimage of Identity*, by David Whyte, whom I'd previously known only for his poetry. "Work," Whyte writes, is "an opportunity for discovering and shaping the place where the self meets the world." Even as we are shaping the work we do, he says, our work is shaping us.

I've always thought I should separate *who* I am from *what* I am, and always disliked the fact that, when I meet people for the first time, one of their first questions is invariably, "What do you do?" (Or now, "What *did* you do?") But this book has me pondering how much the work I've done has made me—shaped me, if you will—into the person I am today.

For most of my working life, I've been, in one form or another, a teacher—a vocation, I now see, I was cut out for. I still remember the jolt of energy I felt my first day of teaching, when I overheard a kid whisper to another: "Hey, he's pretty cool!" And for the next thirty years, seeing faces light up after I'd shown kids something in a Hemingway short story, a Frost poem, or a Shakespearean play was one of the greatest feelings in the world. Right up there with sex.

I can certainly see how I shaped my work, especially during the first half of my teaching career. As head of the English Department at a regional high school on the coast of Maine, I helped instigate and administer a new English curriculum, which included two advanced placement English programs that, one state evaluator said, rivaled the curriculum at Phillips Exeter Academy.

But I've never realized before now how, at the same time I was shaping the curriculum, this curriculum was shaping me. During those years, I created a persona based on the college professors I admired. Driven by the shame of growing up in an alcoholic family, teaching gave me the respect I craved and cultivated. At a time when teachers were dressing more and more informally, I wore suits and vests and ties with matching pocket handkerchiefs. I assigned abstruse literary works by William Faulkner and James Joyce. I covered student compositions with acerbic comments, which more than once reduced school valedictorians to tears.

I became a local legend. And, for a while, I loved it.

Then suddenly I was suffocating. "I have become everything I hate," I wrote in my journal. My teaching persona felt more and more like a body bag. This urge to break out of what seemed like a prison led to the breakup of my marriage, which, ironically, had been weakened over the years by the amount of time I'd spend preparing lessons, correcting compositions, and designing English programs.

Finally, I left school in the middle of the academic year to marry another woman and live in Southern Maine.

Since then, I've often looked back at those fifteen years as misspent, seen myself as phony, blamed myself for hiding behind walls. Overlooking the students from those years who still write to me, I've focused only on the students I failed by not considering a horrific home life or a major learning disability.

Whyte's book has helped me understand those years differently: "…often it is simply the nature of things that walls that once served and sheltered us…only imprison us when we have remained within their confines for too long."

The book also shows me how I broke out of that prison. Whyte talks about our need for "an outlaw figure," an image from our youth to emulate, someone who represents freedom, who seems to live outside society's walls. For me that figure was a composite of the writers I'd been teaching—Hemingway, the Romantic poets, Thoreau—whom I began to understand not as puzzles to be unlocked, but as writers seeking to understand the world around them.

At that regional high school, remembering my own high school dreams of being the next Ernest Hemingway, I started a creative writing elective that became the one place I could catch my breath. After I remarried and found a new high school teaching position, I created another creative writing class, open to all students, so I had special needs kids sitting next to the advanced placement students.

"We must," writes Whyte, "give up exactly what we thought was necessary to protect us from further harm." Whether by accident or grace or something else, I later turned down opportunities to teach senior AP English again and become English Department head, somehow realizing that to put on my old persona would be to sentence myself to life behind bars.

After Laurie's death, I found it harder and harder to teach at the high school level. Driven also by my own need to write, I took early retirement from public education, thinking that my teaching days were over. But to bring in money while I went back to school, I started working in a writing center at a nearby college. I soon came to enjoy working with college students, not seeing myself as a font of wisdom standing in front of a classroom, but as a pair of ears sitting beside them.

Even after receiving my MFA, I continued to work at the writing center for another ten years. During that time, I began to facilitate spiritual writing groups at my church, which I continue to do. Then, after leaving the college job, I started volunteering at a day shelter for the homeless and materially poor. After a month or so there, I started shooting the breeze with a guy I was sitting with. He told me he'd lost his construction job and was living in the homeless shelter. I said I'd been a teacher.

"What'd you teach?" he asked.

"English," I said. "Literature and writing. I really liked teaching creative writing."

"Why don't you offer something like that here?" he said. "I've got a lot I'd like to say."

And so I did "something like that" for the next five years.

Looking back on my career as a pilgrimage, I see that I began teaching by working my damnedest to appear powerful, wise, and in control, and that I'm ending it sitting with others in my spiritual writing groups, all of us "writing to discover" some of this mystery we call life.

So I think Whyte is right when he says that we shape our work and are in turn shaped by the work we have done. If so, I count myself fortunate to have spent my life working at a job I've almost always enjoyed, work that shaped me—may still be shaping me—to become more open and more vulnerable.

"Melancholie" by Albert György

See copyright page for image permissions.

On Emptiness

Gazing at the figure, I felt a physical reaction, a shiver, or perhaps more like the quiver of a struck bell. And I guess I wasn't the only one who resonated to Romanian artist Albert Gyorgy's *Melancolie*: the sculpture went viral on Facebook a few years ago.

I wasn't surprised that many comments came from viewers who'd lost children. A fellow grieving father responded: "We may look as if we carry on with our lives as before. We may even have times of joy and happiness. Everything may seem 'normal.' But *this emptiness* is how we feel…all the time."

Later that same week, I mentioned to an old friend that the hole left in my heart by the death of my daughter would never go away. He seemed surprised and upset. "I had no idea," he said. "I thought because you're a Christian, your faith would sustain you. I feel sorry for you."

No, I wanted to say, don't feel sorry for me. My faith does help me. My life isn't sad. My life is in some ways more joyful than it's ever been. I continue to have a close relationship with Laurie. I—

And as I felt myself thrashing about, frustrated at not having the words to describe what it's like to lose a child, I realized what an intricate and perplexing landscape this emptiness through which I journey really is.

There's the idea of emptiness as void, empty of meaning. It's a frightening place. When my ex-wife phoned me with the news that

The Geriatric Pilgrim

what we'd always thought was a harmless sebaceous cyst on the back of our daughter's head was malignant, I felt the ground opening under my feet. I remember needing to grab on to the counter I was standing beside. Mary Lee has since told me that when I picked her up at school later that day, and she opened the door to the car, she felt an icy emptiness even before I told her the news.

The title of the sculpture, *Melancolie*, or *Melancholy*, refers back to medieval medicine and to one of the four "humours"—black bile—thought to cause what we today call depression. This, too, is a kind of emptiness, at least when I look at some of the therapy websites that define emptiness as "a negative thought process leading to depression, addiction...."—both of which I've stumbled through since Laurie died.

But over those same years, I've also found that emptiness can be something to cultivate rather than cure.

My first readings about emptiness were from existentialists like Albert Camus, who saw meaninglessness as a reality of life, but who posited that we can and should create our own meaning. From there, I dabbled in Buddhism, where emptiness is a central precept. But as I understand it, Buddhists do not believe life is meaningless; rather, that our images of ourselves as separate, independent entities don't exist: they're delusions, empty of meaning. When we can understand this meaning of emptiness, we realize that we are part of what the Buddhist monk Thich Nhat Hanh calls "inter-being," which is the basis for wisdom, bliss, compassion, clarity, and courage.

After my flirtation with Buddhism, I learned a form of Christian meditation called "Centering Prayer," which is based on "kenosis," or "self-emptying." As Saint Paul wrote in his letter to the Philippians: Jesus "emptied himself, taking the form of a slave...." Notice how many of the parables in the Bible advocate giving up everything, whether it's Jesus telling the young man to give up his money and possessions and follow him, or the Good Samaritan giving up his money and time to minister to the man who'd been beaten and robbed, or the servant condemned for burying his one talent.

And it was through practicing kenosis—entering the emptiness I felt after Laurie died, giving up my image of myself as grieving parent—that I was able to feel Laurie's renewed presence in my life.

Lately, I've been working a 12-Step program based on surrender, which I once heard said, "only happens when there's nothing left." Only when circumstances force us to see that all our props, our addictions have not only proved worthless in giving us what we need, but are actually keeping us unhappy, is it possible for us to give them up, empty ourselves of them.

And yet. No matter how much I read about the subject, how often Laurie's spiritual presence fills my emptiness, my daughter's physical absence feels like an amputation.

And maybe that's the price we pay for loving someone. A friend of mine who lost her husband recently sent me the following quotation from Dietrich Bonhoeffer, German Lutheran pastor and theologian:

> *Nothing can fill the gap when we are away from those we love, and it would be wrong to try to find anything. We must simply hold out and win through. That sounds very hard at first, but at the same time, it is a great consolation, since leaving the gap unfilled preserves the bonds between us. It is nonsense to say that God fills the gap. He does not fill it but keeps it empty so that our communion with another may be kept alive, even at the cost of pain.*

So, emptiness for me is another landscape through which I pilgrimage—four steps forward, three steps back, two steps sideways, circling, backtracking. Sometimes the views are bleak and dismal and the path is strewn with the rocks and roots of depression and addiction, but more and more often these days, as I've surrendered my resentments at people long gone from my life, my judgmentalism, my shame over not being perfect, I've seen some magnificent vistas, felt fresh air tickling what little hair I have left, heard birds singing hymns of grace.

Rooting Around

Trees have always called to me, and during this pandemic, I've had a lot of time to read about them. My sister, Jaye, on the other hand, has been using the time to compile a family genealogy. As I think about this, I wonder if what we're both been exploring are roots.

Jaye and I are among the last leaves on our family tree. My only child has died. My brother is gay. My sister's only son and his wife cannot have children. Thus, our family name ends with my brother and me, and our family genes end with my nephew and his wife. So, since Jaye and I are no longer looking ahead, maybe we're looking back at our roots before we dry up and disappear.

Should we care? Are roots all that important?

Of course, trees need them. They survive through their roots. My reading tells me roots can branch out seven times the height of the tree, and that fungi infiltrate roots, not to attack but to partner with them, sharing nutrients across threads that form what's known as a mycelium web—a kind of underground internet, linking roots of different plants, helping one another not only with food, but with information. For example, Jennifer Frazier, writing in *Scientific American*, describes how plants being eaten by herbivores release chemicals that are sensed by neighboring plants, who then increase their defenses.

But what about people? How important is it for us to be aware of our roots?

Well, I think of the trip Mary Lee and I made to Nova Scotia in 2017. I'd always wanted to go to that Canadian province, but it wasn't until my sister discovered that our father's father came from Nova Scotia that I started thinking of turning the trip into a pilgrimage to find roots of my family tree that had previously been buried.

Even when I was a kid, I knew my mother's forebears had lived in our town for generations, but I knew almost nothing about my father's side of the family. Dad's father, Lyman, was a shadowy figure whom no one in our family ever talked about because my grandmother left him when my father was four years old. My sister's research, however, discovered Lyman Beecher Wile had come to this country from the Lunenburg area of Nova Scotia, south of Halifax, in 1906 to work in a shoe factory in Marlborough, Massachusetts. She also unearthed that Lyman's father was named Enoch who'd had two wives, and that Lyman had fifteen brothers and sisters. Going back further, she found that Enoch's family was descended from one Johann Frederich Weil from Germany.

After some sightseeing on Cape Breton, Mary Lee and I drove to Halifax to do more research. Johann Frederich Weil was one of several thousand "foreign Protestants," brought over by the British in 1750 to settle Nova Scotia and to take the place of the French Acadians they were deporting. After three years in Halifax, Johann and his new wife moved to Lunenburg, where his grandson changed the family name to Wile. Following Johann's trail, I discovered south central Nova Scotia is now filled with Wiles: there's a Wileville, a Wile Settlement, a Wile Lake, and several Wile roads. Mary Lee and I spent a delightful afternoon with two other branches of the Wile family whom we met in Wile's Market just outside of Wileville. We spent the next day searching the back roads of Nova Scotia for Enoch Wile's gravestone, which we finally found on a hill looking out past a church steeple and a grain silo toward the rolling, forested hills around a tiny village called East Gore.

I returned from that trip feeling somehow more whole, more sturdy, as if I'd discovered a leg I never knew I had.

But while I'm grateful for having found these roots, I'm also sad because my father never discovered them. After my grandmother had left Lyman Wile, she put her son—named Lester for Lyman's brother who died in the influenza pandemic of 1918–19—into what was called "a Home for Wayward Boys" in Massachusetts until she took him to Maine at the age of twelve when she remarried. Dad, then, grew up without any sense of what I discovered was a huge family tree, and I find myself understanding for the first time that some of his character traits that used to drive me foolish—his negativity, his gluttony, his alcoholism—were probably efforts to fill an emptiness caused by not feeling supported, grounded in a place, having a home—all benefits that knowing your roots can provide.

Compared to him, I've been lucky. Although I've had to work hard in two 12-step programs to heal the scars of growing up in an alcoholic family, at some level I've always known that I had a family and that they would be there if I needed them. I had a father—however spiritually homeless he might have been—who taught me how to play baseball and basketball, and both a mother and father at all my little league games and high school events. After I told my first wife I was moving out of our house, the first thing I did was call my parents to ask if I could stay with them for a while. When Mary Lee traveled from Colorado to be with me, I knew we could stay with my parents until we found a place to live. And after my daughter died, it was buying my father's mother's house in the town in which I'd grown up that provided an anchor in what felt like a tsunami of grief.

So yes, I think roots are important, both for trees and for people, and I lament the fact that the unique mycelium web of Cleaveses, Bennetts, and Conreys, Reeds, Pools, Hitchcocks, and Crocketts, Whitneys, Davises, Rosses, and Hamiltons, Giles Corey—the only accused witch in Salem Massachusetts to have been pressed to death instead of hanged (his last words were supposedly, "More weight!")—Priscilla and John Alden ("Speak for yourself, John Alden"), the Franklins, Densyts, and Mullins, and yes, the Weils/Wiles ends with my nephew and his wife.

But it's helpful to know trees support not only their own species but other species as well. For example, according to Jennifer Frazier, paper birch trees send carbon to Douglas fir seedlings, especially when they are shaded in summer, probably enhancing their survival. In spring and fall, the Douglas firs return the favor when the birches have no leaves. And when Douglas firs begin to die, their roots, through fungi, send food to young ponderosa pine battling to survive.

So I've been trying to grandparent, as best I can, Mary Lee's sons' children by seeing them as often as possible, taking them hiking or sledding or playing ball, losing to them in computer games I don't understand, and showing them how to play dominoes. I'd also like to think that I can nourish others who struggle with addictions, dysfunctional family histories, grief, or aging by sharing stories of the various pilgrimages that have fed me through the years.

Probably one of the purposes of this book, come to think of it.

Thin Places

ONE OF THE BLESSINGS OF PILGRIMAGE IS FINDING YOURSELF IN A "thin place." If you've never heard the term before, it comes from the Celtic spiritual tradition, and there are some lovely definitions: "where earth and heaven brush cheeks," "where the gap between our reality and God's stops feeling wide and uncrossable," "those rare locals where the distance between heaven and earth collapses." There's a Celtic saying: "Heaven and earth are only three feet apart, but in a thin place that distance is shorter."

Poetic as these definitions are, however, they don't explain to me why some places I've visited seem "thin" while other seemingly similar places don't. The island of Iona, off the west coast of Scotland, is for me the "thinnest" place I've ever been, while the Holy Island of Lindisfarne, off the Northumberland coast of England, established by the same monks who settled on Iona, is in my memory just another pretty place. The Desert House of Prayer in Arizona is one of my thin places, while Ghost Ranch in New Mexico isn't. The redwoods in Northern California are; The New Camaldoli Hermitage a few hundred miles south isn't. The chapel of Dominus Flevit on the side of the Mount of Olives is; the Church of the Holy Sepulchre in Jerusalem isn't. Although I have relatives in both places, Riverside Cemetery in Yarmouth, Maine is; the town's Baptist Cemetery isn't.

Thin Places

This isn't to say that I haven't enjoyed visiting these other places, haven't in some cases been transformed by them; it's just that I didn't come away feeling—as I have after being in one of my thin places—as if I'd just stood on some threshold between the secular and the spiritual, glimpsing at something larger, eternal, and loving.

So what do my thin places have in common? They have physical similarities. One is the quality of light. Light on Iona, for example, seems to shimmer, casting heather-covered rocks in an ethereal glow. I love sunlight through trees, whether it be through towering redwoods or the gnarled maple trees over my family's gravesite. While most of my thin places are out of doors, I recall how light shining through stained glass in England's Salisbury Cathedral seemed to take me into another reality.

My thin places are invariably old. The stones on Iona are almost three billion years old. Some of the redwoods Mary Lee and I hiked under were growing when Jesus walked the earth. The giant saguaro cacti in Arizona don't start growing arms until they reach the age of sixty.

For me, a thin place needs to be silent, or at least free of human sounds. I love music, but neither Bach nor Mozart has ever taken me to a thin place; the bleating of sheep on Iona, the mournful howl of coyotes in Arizona have. What so joyously surprised me about hiking under the redwoods was the complete silence. Squirrels and other animals live so far overhead you can't hear them. The same is true of the wind. There aren't any buzzing sounds because one reason redwoods live so long is that they are resistant to insects. And since there are no insects for them to eat, you don't hear any birds.

Water is often found in my thin places: the powerful sensuality of the ocean thrusting into Fingal's Cave off Iona, the *boom*, the withdrawal; the Royal River in Yarmouth winding beneath the Riverside Cemetery, connecting my past to my future. Sometimes the water is in the form of clouds: desert sunrises and sunsets trailing glorious pink and red clouds; huge white clouds nestling just over the ocean.

My thin places inspire kindred states of mind. One is a feeling of vulnerability. Under the height of the redwoods, I feel small and insignificant. Compared with the age of the stones on Iona, or even at Riverside Cemetery, I know I am, as the psalmist says, "like dust," and my days "like grass." But at the same time, I am also comforted. The stones on Iona have seen the formation of continents, the rise and fall of mountain ranges, several reversals of the magnetic poles, and at least five mass extinctions of the world's species. "This, too, shall pass," they sing to me.

When I've been in a thin place, thought seems to fall away, leaving a luminous quality, a "Cloud of Unknowing," as a fourteenth-century monk described it. I am in a place outside of or beyond my five senses. I am unencumbered by ego or false self or monkey mind, or whatever constitutes the buzzing in my head I live with most of the time: the voice telling me I'm God's Gift to the World, the voice proclaiming I'm the Dumbest Piece of Excrement on the Planet, the voice that always wants to ask, "Why?" the voice that cries, "I want! I want!"

I've read thin places result from electromagnetic fields generated by certain kinds of rock, which could certainly be true on Iona. I've also read that a sort of emotional residue left behind by generations of pilgrims makes a place thin. But neither theory explains why not every place touches people the same way. An Episcopal monk I know was more moved by the island of Lindisfarne than by Iona. I saw people at the Church of the Holy Sepulchre in Jerusalem, possibly the ugliest, hottest, loudest place I've ever been, dissolving in tears of spiritual passion. I know a woman who saves all year long so that she can go to Ghost Ranch for a week.

So I have to wonder if these thin places have more to do with us than with physical space. As the Buddhists say, "We see things not as they are, but as we are." Probably the closest I've ever been to the doorway between the finite and the infinite was the night I held my daughter's hand and wiped the mucus from her mouth as she passed over from life to death. So shouldn't Room 434 of the Eastern Maine

Medical Center have been a thin place? I experienced, however, no transcendence into the Eternal, no loving presence, no feeling at all except for that of my own snot and tears.

But I know people who have experienced great peace at the bedside of a dying friend or relative, and I wonder whether each of us isn't hardwired, as they say, to respond differently to different places, different stimuli. (I'm suddenly thinking of my friends for whom music is that doorway into the ineffable.) And if this is true, does that mean that all places can be thin places? Maybe they can. Maybe the purpose of those places we think of as thin (and I'm guessing you have your own places) is to help us realize that God, our Higher Power, the Holy, the Infinite—choose your own word—can be anywhere, if we can learn to open what one writer calls "the eyes of our hearts" and see.

A Pilgrim's Journal: September 23, 2010

Gethsemani Abbey
Near Bardstown, Kentucky

I COME OUT OF THE WOODS AND CROSS MONK'S ROAD TO ANOTHER road that says, NO TRESPASSING. *I'll bet this is it,* I think, and decide I'll be damned if I'm going to travel two thousand miles not to see the hermitage of Thomas Merton, the closest thing to a hero I've had since John F. Kennedy.

When we were first writing to each other, Mary Lee introduced me to Merton's writings, but with my limited Protestant Church background, I didn't understand many of his references, not to mention his Catholicism. Later, I learned some of his story—cosmopolitan young man and promising writer leaves New York, enters the monastery here at Gethsemani, and becomes a Trappist monk—but I still didn't understand much of what he wrote. And when my daughter was lying in the hospital dying from cancer, I hated what I thought I did understand. I remember one night at the Ronald McDonald House reading from *New Seeds of Contemplation:* "All sorrow, hardship, difficulty, pain, unhappiness, and ultimately death itself can be traced to rebellion against God's love for us." Enraged, I threw the book across the room.

Ten years later, however, as I recovered from bilateral hip surgery, I read Merton's autobiography, *The Seven Storey Mountain.* This came at a time when I was starting to feel that, after thirty years in public education, it was time for me to do something else. *But what?* Merton showed me that I should start living the life I wanted to and trust that God would reveal some way to make it work. So I began writing—took a summer workshop, joined a writing group—became more active in my church, started going on spiritual retreats. Then I retired from public school teaching. I found a part-time job as a writing assistant at a nearby college. I worked on my writing, which soon became tied to my discovery of contemplative prayer, where Merton—who is usually given credit for rediscovering the Christian contemplative tradition—became my guide through books such as *Conjectures of a Guilty Bystander, Selected Poems, Wisdom of the Desert,* and *Zen and the Birds of Appetite.* I even reread *New Seeds of Contemplation.*

Now, I've made a pilgrimage to Gethsemani Abbey because I'm again struggling, both with my writing and with the rest of my life. After years of working on a memoir about Laurie's death and my resulting faith journey, I've realized I still don't have the perspective to analyze the experience the way a good memoir should. I've decided to turn the memoir into a novel in hopes of distancing myself from the events as I change them to suit the arc of the story. But someone whose opinion I value wondered recently if I'm not stuck in the past, unable to let go of Laurie's memory and my grief; and I'm worried that he might be right—that I'm wasting both my time and God's with my writing instead of doing something more active such as teaching a class at the state prison, doing more pastoral care, working in a soup kitchen or with parents who've lost children.

So far, this pilgrimage hasn't helped me find any answers. Ever since Mary Lee and I have been at Gethsemani, I've felt like an outsider, a tourist instead of a pilgrim. As a non-Catholic, I haven't been able to take communion. Now, I'm skulking along the side of a narrow dirt road, glancing over my shoulder, planning my excuse if anyone comes along: "Oh, am I trespassing? I didn't see the sign"—because Merton's hermitage, where he wrote so many of his books, is off-limits to visitors.

I'm hot and sweaty. Even in late September, the afternoon temperature here is around ninety degrees. The air smells charred. Leaves on the trees by the side of the road are chewed and full of holes, tinged with brown or black. Storm clouds mass over the burnt-brown hills like an army preparing to drive me back to Maine.

I come to another turnoff, this one marked MONASTIC ENCLOSURE. Do you suppose? I decide not to push my luck and continue going straight until I come to a power line. I follow it and then double back through the woods to a clearing. *Yes!* I recognize the small house with the flat roof and front porch nestled under the trees. I am indeed looking at Merton's hermitage. Wiping the sweat from my eyes, I take several pictures.

I turn to see fields separated by lines of trees and the red barn and pointed chapel tower and round chapel that he wrote about, not far from where I'm standing. I imagine him sitting on the porch, putting pen to paper. I recall how often he wrote about feeling like an outsider, how often he questioned his life, whether he ought to be writing, even whether he ought to be a monk. I feel myself reconnecting to his spirit.

Then I recall yesterday afternoon, as I sat under a tree beside the cemetery of white crosses where Brother Louis, as Merton was called at Gethsemani, is buried, reading an entry in one of his journals in which he writes about how he'd found his "deepest self" through a "creative consent to God."

I wasn't sure what he meant, but this morning I took a walk to "The Statues," along a stone walkway leading to a field, past a lake, and up some wooden stairs to a path through the woods, where I passed a variety of statues—some modern, some traditional—of cherubs, monks, several images of Saint Francis, and a variety of Madonnas. Turning a corner, I saw two statues, one depicting Jesus and the other three of his disciples in the garden from which this monastery takes its name. The disciples (Peter, James, and John?) sleep on some stones, their bodies curled up comfortably, their faces smooth and serene. Farther down the path, however, Jesus kneels on a stone, his head thrown back, his hands over his face, his body wrenched back as if he were a bow waiting for an arrow.

Standing in front of the figure, I felt the tension pulling at Jesus's chest and throat. I recalled those years after Laurie died when I felt alone, betrayed by friends and family and colleagues, experiencing the vast chasm that exists between those who suffer and those around them.

Now, however, standing by Thomas Merton's hermitage, I also sense in those statues, as well as here in Merton's hermitage, a creative spirit rising from the dead grass and the decaying leaves, transcending suffering while at the same time honoring it. I see how art—whether sculpted stone or language—can be a form of resurrection, a way to overcome death by giving it shape. And I realize that by giving shape to my grief, my writing is helping me stay alive: that I can't not write. What may or may not happen to anything I write isn't up to me.

Maybe, I think, this is the kind of "creative consent" Merton was talking about: to create and then consent—turn it over—to God. I hear Jesus's words from that night in the Garden of Gethsemane: "Yet not my will, but yours be done."

Slowly, I head back to the power line. I suppose I should pray, "*Forgive me my trespasses,*" but I'm not sorry. Somehow, in finding Merton's hermitage, I've found something in myself.

The River

Pulled by currents you don't understand, you swing off the interstate at the exit to the small Maine town in which you grew up, turn right off Main Street, and drive down the hill past the house in which you were raised. You park in a small parking lot by the river, high with snow melt-off, the water rushing over the dam, roaring over rocks, spraying mist high into the air.

Behind the dam, fir and pine and maple trees reflect in placid waters, a quintessential New England scene that you remember from your childhood when the river called to you to come and play. When you had no idea the waters carried chicken parts from the factory upriver, tannins from a shoe company, raw sewage from the houses along the shore, and leftover toxins from an old paper company.

As rivers go, the Royal River isn't much—only thirty-nine miles long from its origin in Sabbathday Lake to where it flows through the town of Yarmouth out to Casco Bay. Still, this river, you realize—its beauty, its pollution—has always flowed through your life.

You watch a seagull flying overhead and up the river. In your imagination, you follow it to a natural waterfall where the water bubbles past the remains of the Forest City Paper Company, where your great-grandfather had once been a foreman. He and his wife had been proud people, concerned with their status in town. When his daughter told him she was in love with my grandfather, the son of a local farmer, her father told her, "George is a good man, but you could do better."

Was he right? Had he glimpsed the disease of alcoholism that would pollute the next three generations?

You imagine yourself circling back, flying over the footbridge closer to the dam erected on the site of an old trolley bridge, over which your mother used to walk to school as a girl, carrying the weight of her shame at being the daughter of an alcoholic who couldn't hold a job or pay his town taxes, as well as her dreams of making the town look up to her in admiration.

She succeeded. She single-mindedly raised herself to become a respected member of the community. She filled every position in her church except for pastor. She climbed through the ranks of a large insurance company to become an executive secretary. She was a loving wife to two husbands and devoted herself to her own mother and her three children.

Still, she carried the scars of her childhood. She was a manipulative gossip, often trying to control people behind their backs. She was judgmental of people while craving everyone's approval. Her anger was explosive. With her children, she was domineering, totally oblivious to personal boundaries.

Which brings your mind back to the parking lot below the dam. You're five years old. No parking lot now, just bamboo and burdock. You see yourself in your striped shirt, corduroy pants, and PF Fliers, pretending to struggle through a jungle of lions and tigers, when you look up to see your mother looming over you, her eyes blazing with anger.

You know you're not supposed to be here. Because of the pollution, the rocks, and the rapid currents, your mother has told you over and over never to go down to the river by yourself, but that morning, you'd been bored, so you waited until your mom was in the cellar doing laundry and took off.

Now, here she is, hairbrush in hand: her weapon of choice.

The Geriatric Pilgrim

Rather than freeze in fear or try to run away from what you know is about to happen—what most kids would have done—you start slapping yourself on the rear end, crying, "Mommy, Mommy, you don't have to spank me! See, I can spank myself."

And you still don't know, three-quarters of a century later, whether you did this out of fear of the pain of being spanked or out of the shame of letting your mother down.

All you know is that shame has been the driving force in your life—from grade school when you felt the ridicule of being overweight, to high school when it seemed as if every girl in the halls was laughing at you, to four miserable years in college when everyone seemed to disdain you, to the years after your daughter's death when you knew God had rejected you. You still wake up nights in a sweat, your heart pounding after dreaming of being stripped, tarred and feathered, and ridden on a rail through a crowd of jeering people.

Now, as an eighty-year-old man sitting in a car, peering through a misty windshield, you realize how this river has shaped your imagination, the way you perceive and interpret your life as a river polluted by the shame that has flowed through your grandparents, your parents, and you, churning and spilling its banks.

You gaze again at the placid brown waters above the dam. You remember as an older child swimming in those brown waters, despite the threat of your mother's hairbrush, dogpaddling through chicken parts, dead fish, and raw sewage that drifted down from the upper falls, which from a distance was this white rush of water gamboling over great gray rocks and sending ethereal mist into the air, and you wonder if that's why you go to church, to 12-step meetings, make retreats, go on pilgrimages despite friends' disdain and theological questions that bob like chicken guts—if you aren't paddling along, trying to stay afloat, grateful for the glimpses of grace flowing from the headwaters of your life.

Scars

For fifty years, I've been facilitating writing groups of various kinds. Participants have ranged in age from fourteen to eighty. They've been students, white-collar professionals, blue-collar workers, unemployed, and homeless. Over that time, I've begged, borrowed, or stolen certain writing prompts that always seem to work, no matter who's there. For example, when a group meets for the first time, and I want to avoid the standard introductions and at the same time establish an atmosphere of trust, I'll have us (since I always write, too) write about our scars.

Almost everyone begins by mentioning physical scars. Men, especially, seem proud of them. A few years ago, I was watching a Netflix series called *Longmire*, in which Sheriff Longmire has been stabbed and his female deputy Vic is helping him bandage the wound.

"You've got a lot of scars," Vic says. "How many do you have?"

"Oh, I don't know."

"Come on. All men know how many scars they have."

Silence. Then, "Twelve…thirteen now."

Perhaps it's a sign of the times that women are becoming less reticent about their physical scars. I recall Cosmopolitan magazine photographs of women proudly showing their mastectomy scars. Photographer Ami Barwell said in the press release, "These photographs show that, despite what they've been through, these women are empowered. They are strong, happy, and sexy."

Scars are part of growing up, and in many cultures, children are intentionally scarred when they reach puberty as part of sacred rituals to celebrate their becoming adults. Richard Rohr, whom I often reference in my writing, wonders if the popularity of tattoos and body piercings these days isn't a secular substitute for what young men and women once gained through circumcision, scarification, shaving of heads, and knocking out of teeth.

My most unusual scar is the one on the inside of my right elbow that looks like a burn. I like to show it to people to see if they can guess what caused it. Most can't, because the scar tells not only of my past but also of an era long ago and far away. When I was four years old, I was in the cellar with my mother one day while she was doing the weekly laundry in our wringer washing machine. Fascinated by the rotation of the rollers, I stuck my hand up to touch them. The next thing I knew, I was screaming as the wringers went round and round on my arm—the first of what we in my 12-step program call our "goddamned learning experiences."

As I grew up into something resembling adulthood, I scarred the back of my head when I fell down some school steps onto a broken bottle. I garnered several knife scars from working in a market garden cutting lettuce, spinach, and beet greens, and a black scar when my friend Jerry and I were sword fighting with pencils in a high school chemistry class. (The lead is still in my hand.) Recent x-rays of my scarred lungs remind me of the years in college I worked fighting forest fires, inhaling wood smoke for hours until I could take a break, get away from the smoke, and light up a cigarette.

As an adult, I have a two-inch scar on my back from a fusion of L2 and L3 vertebrae. I have two hernia scars and two longer scars from bilateral hip replacement that I've always thought of as resulting from the time after my daughter died, when, like Jacob, in the Old Testament, I wrestled with angels.

Scars

But if we're proud of our physical scars, we tend, I think, to hide our emotional ones. I've spent seventy years hiding the scars of shame, rejection, and fears of confrontation and failure caused by growing up in an alcoholic family. And Laurie's death has left a scar that feels more like an amputation, one that, even after thirty years, gets ripped open every time I visit someone in the hospital or read in the newspaper about the death of a young person.

For some reason, our physical scars, which almost always are signs that we've failed at something, make us proud, while our emotional scars, which often aren't the result of anything we've done, but rather of things done to us, make us ashamed. Maybe it's because our physical scars say, *I can take it. I'm not a victim. I've survived,* while our emotional scars say, *I should be stronger, more in control.* When Laurie died, I felt weak and powerless. I did not go to her funeral. I refused to run her obituary in the local newspaper. I had recurring dreams about old high school basketball teammates making fun of me for being uncoordinated and slow. In other words, I was ashamed of myself, not because of anything specific that I'd done or not done, but because of who I thought I was: a loser.

As I reach the eightieth year of my earthly pilgrimage, one of my goals is to become as proud of my emotional scars as I am of my physical ones. I'm inspired, as I so often am, by the men and women in my writing groups. As Bill, who lived in the local homeless shelter after losing his construction career job because he'd broken his back and become addicted to pain killers, wrote:

> *Scars are the ledger of life. The reminders of when we lacked experience. Wounds are due to ignorance and inattention, apathy, and sometimes poor coincidence. Some we hide from others, some from ourselves. Some are shared with only a few. Some we display proudly. You would think scars are grievous things. In truth they are wondrous. Scars are badges of life's ills and trepidations…healed.*

Pilgrimage to City Lights

A PILGRIMAGE NEEDS A DESTINATION, A PLACE WHERE, AS ONE writer puts it, God dwells. In June of 2016, my destination was City Lights Book Store in San Francisco, known since 1953 as a literary landmark. Well, okay, it was also Mary Lee's and my thirtieth wedding anniversary, and we had some other sites in mind to visit, but I did want to visit City Lights, because it was a home for the writers who created what was called the Beat Generation—Allen Ginsberg, Gary Synder, Lawrence Ferlinghetti, and the god at whose feet I once worshipped, Jack Kerouac.

Many readers see the road trips in Kerouac's autobiographical novel, *On the Road*, as a series of pilgrimages, whose destination is, as one critic writes, "a limitless pursuit of possibility." Certainly in the early 1960s, as I left adolescence and began stumbling along that dark and mysterious road to adulthood, *On the Road* was a beacon proclaiming that I could achieve anything I desired. A senior in high school, I made up my mind to leave behind the old farts, dumb parents, and dim-witted classmates who lived in the small Maine town in which I'd grown up, and challenge conventional thinking, search out new vistas.

That summer, I left Maine for the first time in my life to visit the Smoky Mountains of Tennessee, and a year later, I found a summer job working on a hotshot crew out of McCall, Idaho, fighting conventionality as well as forest fires. When I returned to the University of Maine the following fall, I continued to pursue an inchoate image of myself as romantic hero—sitting in the back of the Bear's Den in my black Frisco jeans, khaki shirt, and smokejumper boots, disdaining the guys in pinstripes and chinos, the girls in plaid skirts and white blouses, for being weak-spined conformists. I read Kerouac's *The Dharma Bums*, identifying with the protagonist who works in a forest fire lookout tower in the Cascade Mountains of Washington State where I'd been on a fire. I switched my major from forestry to English and decided to become a great writer.

Of course, like so many others of my generation, I was just dabbling in the Beat life. I didn't participate in sex orgies—seldom dated at all—didn't have peyote or mescaline visions (I've never even smoked pot), wasn't rolled through the streets of New York in a barrel. It didn't take more than a couple of years for my dreams of tooling down the road less traveled to wither away in a desert of loneliness, and for me to buy some chinos and pinstriped shirts, get married three days after graduating from college, and become a high school English teacher.

Some twenty years later, however, when that marriage had become sterile and I found myself suffocated by my own pseudo-academic self-image, I reread *On the Road*—lying awake at night remembering the joy of driving across the country at two in the morning, the endless cups of coffee, the third pack of cigarettes that day, my eyes like headlights cutting through the darkness. I began to recognize a spiritual component to the time I'd followed Sal Paradise and Dean Moriarty on the road: the highway stretched out straight and flat before me, my body tingling, free, filled with a combination of joy and longing for transcendent love.

And in some ways, I made the trip to City Lights to honor the thirtieth anniversary of having extricated myself from that first marriage and that self-image and celebrate California with the woman I never would have found if I hadn't bucked conventionality.

I think I made three trips to City Lights before Mary Lee and I left San Francisco, perusing shelves and buying at least a half dozen books, including one by Kerouac I hadn't read, *Big Sur*. Every time I went to the checkout register, I'd give the young women with their dyed black hair, bright red lips, and heavily tattooed pale skin my best Kerouac smirk as they rang me up, as if to say, "Hey, I'm hip, too."

During the next week, after spending my days hiking the holiness of the redwoods with Mary Lee, I read *Big Sur* in the evenings and saw facets of Kerouac I'd not noticed in my earlier life. I realized that what probably attracted me in ways that Allen Ginsberg and William Burroughs and Gary Snyder never did was the lower-middle-class, New England background Kerouac and I shared, as well as a strong, even domineering mother, and our inability to let go of early religious upbringing.

I was also introduced to a Kerouac I'd ignored: Kerouac the alcoholic.

Written some years after the author's best-known works, *Big Sur* is a thinly veiled autobiography following "Jack Duluoz" and his descent into alcoholism after the unwanted fame of his first novel. Using a cabin in Northern California as the focal point, Kerouac details his alcohol delirium tremens, his insecurities, his transient joys, his deep sorrows. Many of the scenes show him to be nasty, self-absorbed, and combative, with occasional bursts of spiritual insight.

I could identify.

The day after Laurie died, I turned the guest room where she used to stay when she visited into a den, in which I spent the next three or four months drinking myself into a stupor and writing nasty letters to my former pastor, Laurie's doctor, and the superintendent of schools at which I taught. I kept a journal in which I railed against the evils of our society, everything from athletes using steroids to students taking drugs to women getting Botox treatments to men popping Viagra. I ignored my wife and her son, shortchanged my students, made biting remarks to my mother and family and old friends.

And yet, unlike Kerouac, who died in his mother's house at forty-seven from a massive abdominal hemorrhage brought on by booze, I was, as I was reading *Big Sur*, seventy-three, relatively healthy and sober.

Pilgrimage to City Lights

In part, I realized, this was because, just as I'd never really been a hipster, I'd never been a full-blown raging alcoholic like Kerouac (or even my grandfather). But one night, as I looked across the room of our California B&B at the woman who endured much of my inebriated nastiness, I suddenly saw more to the story. Phillip Cousineau writes, in *The Art of the Pilgrimage*, "The story that we bring back [from our pilgrimage]…is the gift of grace that was passed to us in the heart of the journey." I didn't know any other way to explain why, in the aftermath of Laurie's death, I'd decided to leave that den, why Mary Lee and I were celebrating thirty years of marriage, how I was continuing to find joy in my life, except through grace.

I certainly hadn't earned it.

And it's this recognition that I took back with me from California, as well as a sense of gratitude for Jack Kerouac which continues to this day. From him, I learned that contempt for conventional thinking is both necessary and healthy and that life needs to be lived with passion. Learned this twice, in fact. But his life also teaches me that nonconformity is healthy only if it is grounded in faith in a higher power and free from solipsism and self-delusion. I'm no expert on Kerouac, but I think those defects of character comprise his tragedy. They're certainly defects I've spent the last thirty years asking God of My Not Understanding to remove.

On Hope

BEING A GERIATRIC MEANS LIVING WITH LOSS. LOSS OF SHORT-TERM memory, of muscle tone, of libido, of friends and family. And I'm learning to accept these losses as part of the natural order of things.

But what I don't want to lose is hope.

It's a challenge. Frankly I've lost most of my hope for this country, at least as a democracy. It's more or less agreed upon that much of the damage we've done to our planet can't be reversed. Racism seems to be as natural a human condition as breathing, and as difficult to stop. While I'm not that distressed about my prospects, I worry about my grandchildren's future.

Ironically, what gives me hope is thinking about my daughter's death. As strange as it might sound, I'm finding the more I look back at the years since Laurie died, the more hopeful I am for my grandchildren and for myself.

I'm not entirely sure where this faith has come from, but so far, I can think of four possible sources, four reasons to give me hope, four legacies I want to pass on to my grandchildren for their futures:

- *The Strength of Family.* I grew up in a family scarred by alcoholism, verbal abuse, and abandonment. Some of those wounds were passed on to me and my siblings, and I'm still in recovery, still realizing how this background has influenced my behaviors over the years, from my own tobacco and alcohol addictions to my arrogant and judgmental attitudes. But the work I've been doing lately in my 12-step program has also shown me that I've reaped the benefits of having two parents who overcame their own hideous childhoods, who loved me, sacrificed for me, and, above all, gave me some of my character traits I'm most proud of, including the strength to overcome the loss of a child.

I want to pass that strength on to my grandchildren.

- *The Dynamic Detachment of Nature.* I've spent some of the most spiritual moments of my life struggling up mountains, sweating in deserts, snowshoeing in bitter cold, and peering through ocean fog. What makes these landscapes spiritual for me is that they make me feel small and insignificant. The ocean is going to break over the rocks whether I'm filled with joy or filled with grief; the sunrise will paint the clouds pink regardless of what happens in Washington. Yes, Nature is filled with death, disease, and violence, but even in death, it teems with life. One of my favorite images from hiking Saint Cuthbert's Way from Scotland to England is of a blown-down tree, its roots exposed. The tree's branches have grown into four new trees rising from the decaying trunk. That force, that instinct to grow and blossom and bloom, drives, I think, all life.

I need to remind myself that force runs through my grandchildren, giving them the power to flourish, no matter what obstacles they may face.

- *The Healing Power of the Arts.* Before Laurie died, about the only writing I'd done was in my journals. I was an academic. My goal was to do more work for the College Board as a consultant. But after Laurie's mother and I divorced, Laurie, who had also been focused on academic studies, swapped her L.L. Bean skirts and blazers for long sweaters and jeans, dyed a pink stripe in her hair, painted her fingernails black, and took up art. She attended summer art programs and, until she became ill, was planning to study art in college. After her death, I began going to summer writing programs, took early retirement from public school teaching, and went back to school for an MFA. Writing helped me identify my feelings and became a way for me to harness my anger and shame by writing a book and then revising it through God knows how many rejection slips. More importantly, writing—like the banjo I wail on and Laurie's watercolor that hangs over my desk—creates an essential order to what often seems, especially after a great loss, a chaotic and meaningless universe.

My grandchildren love to listen to stories, love to tell stories. It's apparently natural for them to build and color and draw pictures. I want to nurture those instincts.

- *The Chuckle in the Dark.* In *A Grief Observed*, popular theologian C.S. Lewis recorded his anguish over the death of his wife. Never intending his words to be published, he railed against God for the suffering and pain his wife had endured, and for the sorrow that was tearing him apart and demolishing everything he'd previously believed about God. Gradually, however, he experienced an "impression which I can't describe except by saying that it's like the sound of a chuckle in the darkness. The sense that some shattering and disarming simplicity is the real answer [to the mystery of suffering and death]."

At least once a year I read from the works of an anonymous fourteenth-century writer who felt that the only way one could experience God was in what he called a "Cloud of Unknowing." Since the loss of my child, my experience of God of My Not Understanding has been through subtraction rather than by addition. I've lost all I ever learned about God, especially the idea that God is some compassionate Superman: all-loving, all-powerful, and all-knowing. And as I've lost those images of God, I've experienced an unfathomable serenity.

I'm still not optimistic about the future of this country. I've read too much history about the rise and fall of empires not to feel that our nation is in decline, if not free fall. But over the last few years, I've discovered a difference between optimism and hope. Hope—for me anyway—is as much about the past as it is about the future. Hope looks back and grieves the reality of death, disease, decline, and destruction, but at the same time, hope gives thanks for a life filled with the grace not only to survive but to thrive.

Which gives me hope my grandchildren will do the same.

Names I've Carried

WHEN I BEGAN WRITING THE "GERIATRIC PILGRIM" BLOGS I ADAPTED for this book, I started hearing from people I used to know in what I call my "other lives." After one blog, when I received a comment from an old high school classmate who called me Ricky, followed by one from a former student calling me Sir, I realized one way to identify those other lives is to look at how people from my past name me.

So far, in thinking about the names I've carried on my eighty-year pilgrimage, I've come up with Rickie, Ricky, Richard, Richman, Wile, Wildman, Twinkle-Toes, Sweetie, Lofty, Rick, Dick, Rich, Maine, Froggy, My Son, My Son the Educated Fool, Mr. Wile, Wile E Coyote, Perfessor, Mr. Advanced Placement, Honey, Officer, Sir, Bro, Brother, Da-Da, Dad, Your Father, You Son-of-a-Bitch, You Shit, My Darling, You Poor Bastard, Pastor, Asshole, Hey You! Gampa, Grampa Rick, Grampa Friday.

* * *

I've often celebrated my birthday by watching the classic movie *Casablanca*. When my mother saw that movie in 1943, she was, in the words of the King James Bible, "with child," and thinking Humphrey Bogart's character, Rick Blaine, looked like my father, decided to name me Richard and call me Ricky, the name I grew up with.

Almost all the boys I knew had an "ie" or a "y" at the end of their name: Willie, Allie, Teddy, Scotty, Dougie, to name just a few. The website "English Language & Usage Stack Exchange" suggests this practice dates from Middle English and denotes familiarity, intimacy, or tenderness—all feelings I was graced to grow up with. But by the time I was eighteen, I thought my name childish, a symbol of being overprotected, hemmed in. I wanted to be the Rick of *Casablanca*, the mysterious figure lurking in the shadows of Morocco, sucking on his unfiltered Camels, nursing his whiskey and his deep, dark past and, of course, his love for the beautiful Ilsa. The Camels and the whiskey led to what is now "moderate" COPD and a few battles with booze before I surrendered to a 12-step program. Still, I think that like Bogart's Rick, I am, in the words of Inspector Renault, "a sentimentalist," hiding behind a veneer of sarcasm. I also like to think I have Rick's integrity and concern for the underdog. I do know that one of the first things I noticed when I met Mary Lee was how much she looked like Ingrid Bergman.

* * *

I'll never forget the first time a student called me Mr. Wile. I didn't know who the hell he was talking about. But as other students called me by the same name, I began to experience a pride, a sense of importance, an authority I'd never had before. N. Scott Momaday writes in his memoir, *The Names*, that Native Americans receive names so that they might grow into them. This is what I did with my new name. I became that authority figure—stern, demanding.

One summer, almost twenty years after becoming Mr. Wile, my first wife, our daughter, and I went to a local Fourth of July parade. I ran into some former students, now in college. They said nice things about how well they were doing in English, how thoroughly I'd prepared them for college expectations. I wished them all the best, lit my pipe, and blew a self-satisfied smoke ring. Above the clamor, a voice cried, "Hey, Mr. Wile!" I looked around for another student. I heard the voice behind me: "Mr. Wile?" Turning, I saw my daughter Laurie—she was probably twelve at the time—her eyebrows raised, her forehead furrowed. "I've been saying 'Dad' for the last five minutes," she said, "but you never noticed me."

My God, I remember thinking, *is "Mr. Wile" all I am, even to my own child?* Of course, that wasn't the only reason I quit the Rotary Club, the church board of deacons, my job, and my marriage, but it became an easy reason to point to. And when Laurie died six years later, my guilt and shame over the memory of "I've been saying 'Dad' and you never noticed me" pounded in my chest like one of the monsters in the *Alien* movies that were so popular at the time, threatening to explode and tear me apart.

* * *

Most of the names I've carried have come from other people, but there was one name I gave myself.

About eight years after Laurie died, at a time when I thought that I'd gone through the worst of my grieving and Mary Lee and I were finally starting to enjoy life again, I had a period of darkness such as I hadn't experienced since the first months after my daughter's death. I became withdrawn, angry all over again, and bitter, especially with other people who talked about having suffered a great loss in their own lives. In talking with Mary Lee, my rector, and my spiritual director, I began to see—and I've since read this is common with a great grief—that what I was grieving was not the death of my daughter, but the loss of my grief over the death of my daughter. Without knowing I'd done so, I'd given myself the name "Grieving Father." At some level, I knew I had to lose this name if I were to move on with my life, but at the same time, I didn't want to let it go.

* * *

After starting to write for publication, I couldn't decide what name to put on my work. Should I use *Rick,* as I am called by everyone who knows me these days? Or should I go with the more formal *Richard,* a name I didn't even know I had until I entered school? I saw that most of my mentors wrote under their formal names, and that my formal name was on all my important documents. Besides, I decided, authors calling themselves Rick seemed too new agey, especially for someone of my generation. I went with Richard.

But honestly, I feel like I'm using an alias.

*   *   *

When both of my stepsons and their wives announced that they were going to be parents, I had mixed feelings. I was delighted for them, but at the same time, while not bitter, I was apprehensive about becoming bitter. I will, I told myself, never have a "real" grandchild of my own. These children will already have two grandfathers. Will I be extraneous? The ghost of Mr. Wile whispered in my ear, *You never spent enough time with your daughter. Are you going to avoid your grandchildren, too?*

All of which changed the moment I held first John and then, six weeks later, Anastasia in my arms. All my baggage, all the solipsistic crap melted in the depth of their eyes.

And now I'm some form of *Grampa* to five grandchildren, a name I prize.

For many years, I equated my various names with what Thomas Merton, Thomas Keating, Richard Rohr, and others call "false selves." I felt these names kept me from realizing my "true self," myself as the image of God, "manifested," as Father Keating says, "in our uniqueness."

But these days, I'm wondering if all these names I've carried on my pilgrimage aren't various facets of my true self—don't, in fact, reveal my uniqueness. Madeleine L'Engle writes somewhere that to name something is to assign it meaning, value, importance, and significance. That essentially to name something is to love it. If so, my names, even those reminding me of how love can die, show me that my eighty-year pilgrimage has largely been one through love.

Something worth remembering.

Here Comes the Judge!

THOSE WHO WRITE ABOUT THE PILGRIMAGE EXPERIENCE AGREE that pilgrimages are about traveling light, leaving old patterns of behavior behind, opening yourself to new gifts. And I've done pretty well. Except for the Judge. No matter where I've been, I haven't been able to leave the bastard behind.

I'm in the Church of the Holy Sepulchre in Jerusalem, or Salisbury Cathedral in England, or Iona Abbey in Scotland, magnificent emblems of the holy, and all I notice are the tourists around me following guides like schools of mackerel. Instead of paying attention to God, I hear a voice admonishing, *Aren't you glad you're not one of **them**?*

Or on retreat, in search of silence and serenity at some monastery, I watch the brothers, envious of how much more at peace they seem to be than I am, and hear, *Why can't you be that centered? Maybe if you shaved your head the way the monk over there has, you'll achieve union with God.*

Or hiking through the woods or climbing a mountain, trying to become one with nature, I sense someone behind me on the trail. I glance over my shoulder and see a guy who looks like he's carved from the side of this mountain. *He's catching up with you,* the Judge says. *You have to go faster!* I try to pick up my pace. Stepping aside only when I absolutely have to, I watch the guy stride past and listen to the voice behind my right ear, soft but certain, slow and confident—a lot like Clint Eastwood's: *Why can't you look like that guy?*

I've certainly tried. Over the years, depending on whom I've wanted or not wanted to be, I've gone on diets; I've changed haircuts, grown and cut off sideburns, goatees, shaped beards, and Grizzly Adams beards; I've taken up—and given up—cigarettes, pipes, cigars, snuff, scotch, gin, bourbon, handcrafted beers, jogging, weight-lifting, several religions, a number of meditation techniques, Tai Chi and Qigong, yoga, scraping my tongue, neti pots, and hanging upside down.

The Judge remains unimpressed.

Besides pilgrimages and retreats, he's most likely to show up when I'm in social situations, such as class reunions, church coffee hour, and parties. At my side, he leans in, pointing up at some people with envy, pointing down at others with disdain or pity, as if he and I were viewing them on a stairway.

He was a powerful presence in the times when my life most seemed in chaos. During my first two years of college, when I had no idea of who I was or where I was going, the Judge sat with me in the back of the college Den, disdaining the frat boys and sorority gals for being conformists, while telling me not to go back to my dorm because it was filled with losers. And after Laurie died, the Judge convicted me of murder, sentenced me to a lifetime of guilt because I'd caused Laurie's death, either because I'd left her mother for another woman or because I hadn't left her mother soon enough.

I suspect the Judge was appointed by my alcoholic family, where "What will the neighbors think?" served as the household mantra. Judging is a way to keep people and situations at a distance. If I'm judging people, I'm not vulnerable to what they may say or do. I can barricade myself behind the Judge's bench above the rest of the court, distant, respected, sarcastically wielding my gavel.

Never mind that the Judge has often kept me from being fully present to people, to the beauty of the world around me, to joy.

The Geriatric Pilgrim

* * *

Still, if you go on enough pilgrimages, something is bound to rub off. Several years ago, when Mary Lee and I were traveling on Cape Breton Island, Nova Scotia, the Judge would point to the bony bicyclists pushing themselves up and down the rugged hills, and tell me that when I got home, I needed to lose ten pounds (fifteen would be better). *You ought to get one of those racing bikes,* he said, *or start walking ten miles a day.*

For some reason—I'd like to think it was the grace that can come on a pilgrimage—instead of reacting immediately, I thought, *Well, the Judge usually shows up when I'm self-conscious or anxious about something. What's been going on in my life lately*? All right, I've been dealing with mortality in one way or another all year. Since April, I've seen three people my age die, and several more go into the hospital for major surgery. Could it be that I'm apprehensive about my own death and think that if I could just look like those healthy bicyclists, I might not die, at least not yet, and well, maybe I ought to get my neti pot out again....

And suddenly, the idea that I could diet my way to eternal life was funny. I thought of the old Rowan and Martin television show, *Laugh In*, and Sammy Davis, Jr., dressed in a long white wig and black robes, swinging his arms and strutting like a turkey, crying, "Here come da judge! Here come da judge! Here come da judge!" (If you want to see for yourself, go to YouTube.)

Later that afternoon, as Mary Lee and I walked a trail along the Cape Breton shore, instead of the other mantras I sometimes used when I walked, I breathed in, "Here comes..." breathed out, "the Judge...." Breathed in, "Here comes..." breathed out, the Judge." I might even have strutted a little.

I didn't hear much from him the rest of the trip.

The Judge and I have a much better relationship these days. As long as I don't take him too seriously. I've come to accept him as being like the voice I know alcoholics hear, urging them to take just one little drink. They know that voice will never go away, which is why all the alcoholics I know refer to themselves as "recovering," and not "former" alcoholics.

Which helps me see myself as a "recovering judge-aholic."

Say that three times fast, without giggling.

The Pattern of Exodus

THE FIRST TIME I EVER HEARD THE WORD "EXODUS" WAS PROBABLY in Mrs. Raynes's Sunday school class back around 1950, when we learned about the miracle—Mrs. Raynes was big on miracles—of Moses parting the Red Sea and leading the children of Israel to the Promised Land. A few years later, like half the civilized world, I saw Cecil B. DeMille's *The Ten Commandments*, and learned that Moses looked like Charleton Heston, turned wooden staffs into snakes, and wandered around the desert for forty years.

I thought of the word recently after reading Margaret Gunther's *Walking Home: From Eden to Emmaus*, meditations on famous walks in the Bible. Gunther reminded me that the Israelites had first come to Egypt from Canaan to seek sanctuary from a famine that was sweeping the area. Some of you may remember the story of Joseph, son of Jacob, whose brothers sold him into slavery in Egypt, but who rose to power, becoming Pharaoh's right-hand man. In an act of forgiveness, Joseph invited his father and his eleven brothers to join him in relative comfort while the rest of the area was starving. Four hundred years later, however, the Egyptians had enslaved the descendants of Jacob until Charlton Hcs—I mean, Moses—came to their rescue and led them to the land God had promised them.

What intrigued me was Gunther's observation that this pattern of

The Pattern of Exodus

exodus—from sanctuary to slavery to escape to arrival at the Promised Land—is an archetypal journey many of us take.

My mind traveled to the sanctuary that was my hometown, but which became, by the time I was seventeen, a prison I could hardly wait to escape. In college, I wandered a desert of unhappiness and confusion, until I found what seemed at the time, a promised land in Down East Maine. I recalled a marriage that began in 1965 as a sanctuary from a hostile world's assassinations, civil unrest, and a war that was killing off my friends, only to become in 1985 a passive-aggressive battle with a woman I didn't know and skirmishes with addiction and self-flagellation, before an escape to the promised land of Mary Lee's love and understanding.

Then my thoughts rambled over to when, seeking sanctuary after Laurie died, I bought my grandparents' house back in the town in which I'd grown up—the town I couldn't wait to leave thirty years earlier. At the time, I would have told you that buying the house was like the Israelites crossing the Jordan River into the Promised Land after forty years of wandering.

Adrift in a sea of uncertainty and sorrow, the house became my anchor. Looking into its history, I discovered it had been moved a quarter of a mile from Main Street, that it had been built up, added on to, partially torn down, and remodeled countless times: a mirror, I felt, of what had happened to me over the years. I researched many of the people who had owned my house, found their gravestones, and discovered that almost all of them had lost children, which gave me the comfort of not being alone in my grief. The large maple tree in my backyard became my family tree, complete with a large broken limb jutting from the top.

I assumed I would live in that house until I died.

I'm not sure when this promised land turned to prison. There might have been a foreboding as early as when Mary Lee and I first moved in and I was in the process of turning what had been my grandparents' dining room into my office. To have more space for my books, I was taking off the door to what had been a china cabinet, when I heard my grandfather's voice: *"And what do you think you're doing, young man?"*

Whether because I was afraid of pissing him off even more, or because I found the memories I had of the house comforting (this was the first house I lived in with my mother and grandparents after coming home from the hospital in 1943 while my father served in the Army overseas, the house I came to for Thanksgiving and Christmas and Easter dinners), I left the house largely the way I remembered it, including drafty windows, worn linoleum, and a damp cellar that frequently flooded after storms. I never could call the house "my house" without feeling as if I were lying. The house was always—and remains so in my mind—the house of my grandparents.

One day, shortly after the cellar had flooded again, I realized that I knew more people in the cemetery than I did in the local grocery store. That I was spending almost every day driving to another town because that's where my job, my friends, and my church were. That my anchor had become a millstone.

Still, it took retirement and the recognition that Mary Lee and I were going to have trouble keeping up the mortgage payments and the increasing taxes to spur us to move. Even then, leaving the house was one of the hardest things I've ever done. I remember walking through the empty house after the movers had left, listening to the echoes of footsteps and memories, wondering if I had made a terrible mistake.

But since then, I've never regretted leaving. Have I found the promised land? It depends what *promised land* means, I guess. Certainly, compared to the hundreds of thousands of people being forced these days into exodus from their countries, I have. I'm happy where Mary Lee and I live. Still, I doubt it's permanent. We're trying to budget our bucks so that, if necessary, we'll be able to afford one of the assisted living facilities that have sprung up like mushrooms around here. But they're not going to be any kind of promised land, either.

Growing older, I find myself thinking of the promised land as more of a frame of mind, a spiritual, not a physical, destination, not unlike pilgrimage—a place of freedom from bondage, a place of growth, and at the same time, a place of serenity—a word I'm coming to value more and more these days.

For now, I seem to have found it, but I expect that part of the archetypal pattern of exodus is that one never really gets to the promised land and stays there, at least not in this lifetime. (The Israelites were forced into exile in the sixth century BCE and again in 70 CE.) I expect that I've got one or two more exoduses ahead of me before the big one.

A Pilgrim's Journal: March 19, 2011

New Orleans, Louisiana

I'M SIGHTSEEING IN THE FRENCH QUARTER OF NEW ORLEANS WHILE Mary Lee attends a conference of Episcopal deacons. It's Saint Joseph's Day, a day to honor the Blessed Mary's husband and Jesus's earthly father, whom, as a stepfather myself, I admire and whose Feast Day gives me an opportunity to eat dessert during the six-week penitential season of Lent. Except in a few places around the world, the day is not widely celebrated, but one place that does the day up big is New Orleans, where, as I read this morning, festivities go back to the late 1800s, when Sicilian immigrants settled in the Big Easy.

Which is why I happen to see a parade, hosted by the American Italian Marching Club: hundreds of very large men in sunglasses, tuxedos, and Mardi Gras beads riding on floats, some of them featuring obscene signs, others filled with young girls from Catholic schools dressed in white, with red, green, and white stoles. I see two different wedding parties dancing down the street, as well as a variety of devils in skin-tight leotards. I watch most of the parade standing on Bourbon Street, which has to be the loudest place I've ever been in my life. In addition to the bands passing by, every door to every bar and strip club is open, every band inside is playing, and every third person is screaming at the top of their lungs.

If this is Lent, I think, what's New Year's Eve like?

A Pilgrim's Journal: March 19, 2011

But this afternoon, I visited the exhibit at the Louisiana State Museum: "Katrina: Before, During, and After." I can't recall anything that has made me literally weep for the suffering caused and endured by humanity. That the city could still celebrate anything is a bit of a miracle. (Miracles, by the way, are the reason the Sicilian immigrants celebrate Saint Joseph's Day: apparently Saint Joseph miraculously prevented a famine from ravaging Sicily during the Middle Ages.)

Noise, drunkenness, saints, miracles. I'm befuddled.

* * *

Growing up in a small Maine town in the 1950s, I was inculcated with what Richard Rohr calls "dualist thinking." Things are either good or bad, strong or weak, beautiful or ugly, spiritual or profane, for me or against me. I learned to divide the world into teams of Us versus Them: in the newspapers and on TV, I read about red-blooded Americans versus dirty commies; on Saturday afternoons I saw movies with white hats fighting black hats; and Friday nights on the basketball court, there were the golden boys of our school versus the evil SOBs of the school in the next town.

The older I get, however, the more aware I am that America is not always "good," opponents are not always "bad," and might does not always make right. Nowhere was this truer than after Katrina hit New Orleans. Separating the good guys from the bad is well-nigh impossible. From the media I heard terrible stories of looters running wild, gang rapes, wanton murders by both the local residents and police, even cannibalism. I also read about residents feeding and housing and clothing their less fortunate neighbors, of people risking their lives to evacuate residents from flooded buildings, and of thousands of Americans spending their own money to travel to New Orleans and work eighteen-hour days to help the city rebuild. I heard about a corrupt city bureaucracy struggling to stay in power, incompetent engineering, and a deaf federal government. I also learned about local groups such as the Neighborhood Empowerment Network Association and the Holy Cross Neighborhood Association organizing residents in relief efforts.

Still, I want to ask: which version of what happened is true?

* * *

And then, standing in front of a small club on Bourbon Street, the music takes me "home" to the house in which I grew up. I was surrounded by music. My mother always had either the radio or the record player on. My grandmother played piano for the silent movies in the 1920s, and led her own band (The Charmers) during the '30s. Before Elvis Presley came along, I loved New Orleans jazz—Dixieland, we called it. Even after Elvis, I played trombone in a group called the Ivy Leaguers. We performed at local grange halls, school talent shows, even on a local television show, *Youth Cavalcade*—wailing away on Dixieland favorites such as "Wang Wang Blues," and "Jada" ("Jada, jada. Jada, jada, jing, jing, jing"). These days, I jam with my banjo in local old-time music sessions.

And it's in music, music that I first heard at home, and today everywhere in New Orleans, that I find a way to understand how one can shift from dualistic—"either...or"—to nondualistic—"both...and"—thinking, to learn to see things—things like Truth—as interconnected, like musical notes.

In music, there is no "either...or," only "both...and." Listen to Louis Armstrong and his All-Stars. Armstrong was one of the greatest musicians who ever lived. But what would have happened if the rest of his band had all played the same notes he did? Although the result could have technically been called music, I suppose, it would have been bad music. Each musician, however, in Louis's band played their own notes—sometimes when Louis did, sometimes when he didn't. The harmonies, the syncopation are what turned what they played into jazz. And the same principle holds true in a Mozart symphony. We don't sit there trying to figure out who's playing the "right" notes or who's playing the "wrong" ones.

A Pilgrim's Journal: March 19, 2011

New Orleans, I realize, like all of us, is a symphony of purity and obscenity, selfishness and compassion, joy and grief—only it's more evident, which helps me see that, while my trip here didn't start out as a pilgrimage, I've made what feels like a sacred Lenten journey.

Sunday Afternoon Drives

THE OTHER DAY, WHEN I GOT A NOTICE THAT MY CAR NEEDED ITS next scheduled service, I realized that, whether because of the pandemic or my increased age, I don't drive as often or as far as I used to. Which got me thinking about a forgotten era in my life—in the life of many geriatrics, I suspect—the Sunday afternoon drive.

For me, this era lasted from the late 1940s, when my parents bought their first automobile, to the mid-50s, when the advent of television and Sunday afternoon sports kept my friends and their parents at home. During that time, on Sunday afternoons from spring into the fall, anywhere from three to seven families—the Wiles and the Prides and the Loomises, the Rollstons and the Haskells, the Teffts and the Jameses—would pile into their cars and spend the afternoon traveling the back roads of Southern Maine to places like Blackstrap Hill and Pleasant Mountain to look at foliage, Two-Lights and Reid State Parks to see the surf, and Sebago and Crystal Lakes to swim. Sometimes, we'd just take off and head into what I still think of as Maine's Bermuda Triangle: a series of labyrinthian back roads that no matter which one we took always somehow ended up at a reed-infested body of water called Runaround Pond.

Every one of these families had a kid close to my own age, and it was great fun swapping parents, so I could ride in a car with Craig or Richie or Peter. Some parents were more lenient than mine and let us roughhouse or yell or sometimes sing, which made me feel like I was playing hooky from school; other parents were more strict, making us sit still and whisper, which made me feel like my own parents weren't so bad after all.

Watching all these parents interact gave me my first glimpse into the confusing world of being an adult. I couldn't understand why all the men and most of the women puffed on cigarettes, filling the cars with smoke and stinging our eyes. They often spoke in a strange sort of code that I didn't understand and laughed at things that made no sense.

(Eventually, I learned that many of these comments had to do with sex. I remember what might have been the earliest "dirty" joke I ever heard—although it took me a while to figure it out:

Question: Who was the first carpenter?
Response: Adam?
Answer: No, Eve. She made Adam's banana stand.)

And I find that some seventy years later, my parents and their friends still seem to me to belong to a mysterious world beyond my understanding, a world now lost to me forever. When I browse through the three-by-three-inch, black-and-white photos in my mother's old albums, these people appear older than their children did at the same age: in their forties, they look to be in their fifties and sixties—probably the result of the cigarettes they smoked and the fatty foods they consumed (my father started the day with eggs and bacon right up until he died at sixty-six), but also probably because, compared to today, they look dressed up. Men wore ties, some even on Sunday afternoon drives, and for the most part women wore dresses.

Compared to today, our mothers seldom used profanity and our fathers used a lot less when we were all together. And the "f-word" was rare even in a group of men. On the other hand, all our parents peppered their language with racial and cultural slurs, with epithets for Blacks,

French Canadians, Italians, indigenous peoples, gays, even Catholics. I could get my mouth washed with soap for saying "goddamn," but no one did anything except chuckle if I called John Nappi a wop.

All our parents were affiliated with either the Congregationalist or Baptist Church in town, but except for my parents and the Haskells, the other families usually attended church only on Christmas and Easter. Their real religion was the United States of America. (It was during this time that "under God" was added to the Pledge of Allegiance.) One Memorial Day—I was probably seven or eight—I was walking down the street carrying a full-sized American flag over my shoulder, and Earle Pride yelled out the door of his store at me because the tip of the flag was dragging on the ground.

And if their religion was the United States, they worshipped the American Dream. New washing machines and dryers, larger television sets and hi-fi record players, pine-paneled rec rooms, and most of all, new automobiles. It was common to trade in for a new car every couple of years or so, and when one of our parents did, the car became an object of veneration for weeks, with all us kids scrambling to ride in it on Sunday afternoons.

Those afternoon drives then became a worship service, celebrating our parents'—all of whom had grown up during the Depression—rise into American's great Middle Class, with the freedom to follow new roads to a brighter foliage or higher surf or a longer beach. And if they got lost or suddenly found themselves back at Runaround Pond, well, there was always next week.

It's easy for me to criticize their provincialism and bigotry (and later in life, I did), but maybe because I'm older than most of those men ever got to be, or maybe because I'm aware that I don't have the goals, the dreams I used to have, I find I miss the energy, the—excuse the pun—drive of those people in the black-and-white photographs.

I also realize I miss the faith I had back then in my parents and their friends. Before the advent of Elvis and the generation gap, I believed in them more than I believed in God.

Sunday Afternoon Drives

I remember one Sunday drive that must have been in the late 1940s when forest fires burned large parts of Maine. One of our parents heard that there was a large fire in Brunswick, so we all piled into the cars to go look. I don't remember the fire, only that as we turned the cars around to head back home, I was in the back seat of Earl Pride's powder-blue Dodge with Earl's son Craig. One minute we were horsing around, and the next minute Craig was gone, the back door of the Dodge swung open. Earl slammed on the brakes. I looked behind and saw the other cars screeching to stops. Doors opened and parents rushed to Craig, who was still rolling in the gravel beside the road. My stomach rose into my throat leaving a great empty cavern, until I saw Earl lift his screaming son into his arms, bring him back to the car, and lay him beside me in the back seat. "He'll be okay," he told his wife, Doris, "just some scrapes and a bump on the head." And Earl was right. Because he was just starting to accelerate when the door opened, the car wasn't going that fast. But as far as I was concerned, Craig was never in any real danger. Once his father had him in his arms, I knew he'd be fine.

Like me, Craig has had heart surgery, but all things considered, we're both doing pretty well. Still, other friends have gone this year, some of them almost as suddenly as when Craig disappeared from his father's powder-blue Dodge. It seems as if one minute they're here, the next minute they're not. And I find myself searching for some older, wiser voice, telling me that everything's going to be fine.

Pilgrimage to Riverside

I'VE READ THAT ONE OF THE MOST COMMON PILGRIMAGES IS THE graveside visit. Just about all the strands of pilgrimage are present: the call to leave ordinary life, the need to pay homage, the crossing of a threshold, the act of sacrifice or penance, the return home. As I've written earlier in these pages, pilgrimage also thrusts me into what seems to be another time zone, somewhere between past and present and future. Which is certainly true whenever I drive across that threshold between the two stone pillars shaded by maple trees at the entrance to Riverside Cemetery in Yarmouth, Maine. I can feel my body chemistry change.

Entering the cemetery, I never fail to notice how far it has expanded. Where once there was a market garden in which I used to work—planting, cultivating, and harvesting beet greens, spinach, lettuce, cucumbers, and squash—marble and granite stones now grow in evenly spaced rows. Even more jarring is that the stones lie under trees at least twenty years younger than I am, and which now stand some seventy-five to a hundred feet high.

As I drive around to the back of the cemetery overlooking the river, I pass the newer stones, with laser prints of cars, boats, dogs, even photographs, and then by the older, lichen-dotted marble, granite, and slate stones that feature names I always put faces to: Snap Moxcey, my old barber; Frank Knight, my little league coach;

Red Beal, my eighth grade teacher and coach; parents of many of my former classmates.

In the back of the cemetery, under the ancient maple, I park the car in front of our family lot and get out. I pull a few dead blossoms from the impatiens around my mother's grave. I straighten the American flag in the VFW marker by my father's flat bronze memorial and then move over to clean the sticks and dead grass from the memorial stone for my daughter, who died three years after Dad. Just up from Laurie's stone, a similar granite stone honors my Grandmother Cleaves, who died less than a year after my daughter.

A year before Dad died, Hurricane Gloria knocked out power in parts of Maine for up to two weeks. I was living Down East at the time, and the day after the storm, I got up early to drive Laurie to church camp in the middle of the state for the weekend. After dropping her off, I drove on to visit my mother and father, and when I pulled into the driveway, I saw Dad standing in strewn leaves and fallen branches, trying to fry bacon and eggs on a charcoal grill. Nanny Cleaves, who'd come over from her apartment for a hot breakfast, stood at the window.

What I think of as "pilgrimage time" can not only expand memories but also compress them. The deaths of my father, my daughter, and my grandmother in less than four years become one moment that I recall as an emotional hurricane that made Gloria feel like a summer breeze.

I walk to the center of our lot, to the granite stone from the old cellar hole of my mother's grandparents' house. I clean up a little more, knowing full well that probably no one will ever notice but me. Cemeteries, of course, are for the living, not the dead: a way to show respect, certainly, but also to concretize the great mystery of death—shape it in stone, decorate it.

It took me three years after Laurie's death to realize the healing power of cemeteries. She had not wanted to be buried; she'd wanted her ashes scattered. Once she died, however, her mother was adamant that she wanted our daughter's ashes buried in her family's plot in Steuben, Maine. Reeling from Laurie's death, I couldn't handle any more confrontation, so I said to go ahead, but that I was not going to go to any funeral, would not attend any graveside services. But three years of spending Memorial Days in this cemetery planting flowers, and summer evenings tending them, and autumn afternoons taking away pots and the St. Francis statue my brother, sister, and I added made me realize that Laurie needed to be here as well.

No, that's not right. I realized that *I* needed Laurie to be here as well.

The name WILE is etched on a bronze plaque on the creviced surface of the stone that once was part of the foundation of the old family homestead. This granite is thousands of years old, yet as with the rest of us, time will eventually wear it away. Still, it won't be in my time, not in what I've heard called chronos, or human time.

No, these stones, this cemetery, make me aware of what's called kairos, God's time. I recall the lines from the Isaac Watts hymn I once sang growing up in Yarmouth: "A thousand ages in Thy sight/Are like an evening gone..." And maybe that's what pilgrimages do: help us to leave, even briefly, ordinary time and experience God's time.

Just behind our lot, a tree-covered bank overlooks the river that gives this cemetery its name. The Royal River flows into the harbor and then on a mile or so to Casco Bay. As many writers have noted (including, again, Isaac Watts: "Time, like an ever-rolling stream...."), time is also a river, and standing on the bank, I imagine the Royal River swirling past the house my parents lived in when Hurricane Gloria struck, down over the waterfall by the house in which I grew up, and into the boatyard where my parents kept their little sixteen-foot boat—the boat Mom gave me when Dad died, the boat Laurie liked to go out on before she died. I look down at the channel cutting through lead-colored banks of mud. I watch a cormorant fly down the river and disappear around the bend toward the bay and the ocean, where I can see my father, my mother, and my daughter in that tiny boat, waiting for me to join them.

Have Snakeskin, Will Travel

OVER THE PAST THIRTY YEARS, I'VE MADE MANY RETREATS TO monasteries. The silence, punctuated by worship several times a day, slows me down, increases my awareness, and keeps me centered. All of which have helped me live comfortably through over two years of COVID-enforced isolation.

But as much as I love monasteries, I've never had any desire to be a monk. There's the celibacy thing, for one thing, but also the fact that, at least in the monastery I'm most familiar with, the brothers clean out their cells every year, discarding everything but the essentials. As one brother wrote, "Refraining from possession helps us remember the transient nature of earthly life."

Well, I'll admit it. I want my possessions. The room in which I'm writing this is full of them. I have bowls of stones from the various pilgrimages Mary Lee and I have made, a hat covered in hat pins from states and countries I've been to, and a budding collection of banjos. I also have random things: a wooden plate made by my father, joke books written by an old friend who recently died, a pencil holder that used to belong to my father-in-law....

And a snakeskin.

Almost sixty years old, the skin rests on my bookcase, brittle, brown, and bent. When I pick it up, it crinkles like old parchment. Some of the translucent scales underneath, resembling fragments of old Scotch tape, have fallen off (another came off just now). I can't think of anybody who'd want the damn thing except me. And I wouldn't part with it for a thousand dollars.

As I run my fingers over the mottled brown-and-yellow skin, the years fall away, and it is the summer of 1963. I am slowly coming down a steep slope of something between a hill and a mountain in the Payette National Forest in Idaho. Below me is the third fork of the Salmon River. (Often called "The River of No Return." If you can, check out the 1954 film of that name starring Robert Mitchum and Marilyn Monroe.) As I descend, picking my way through blackened rocks and burned shrubs and grass, I begin to encounter small groves of ponderosa pine and Douglas fir, which I check to make sure aren't smoldering. But they're fine. The fire didn't get down this far.

I'm working on a hotshot crew based in McCall, Idaho, a small touristy town on the edge of Payette Lake (something like five thousand people and eight bars) about thirty miles from here. Our crew is a regional one, which means we're flown to any state in the upper western United States that has a large forest fire. The term "hotshot" describes those who work on the hottest part of a forest fire. Our primary job is to dig a fire line around the fire. We have a crew of eighteen, plus a crew chief, Paul; an assistant crew chief, Tex; and a scout, Dave Bodley—"Bo Diddly," we call him—a bear of a guy who goes ahead with a chainsaw, cutting down limbs, clearing a path through fallen trees. Then, we follow in a line as close to the fire as we can get. Twelve of us carry Pulaskis, a tool that combines an ax and a hoe in one head on a three-foot handle, to scrape the forest duff and chop roots. The remaining six of us have shovels to scrape and widen the fire line to about three feet or more. The idea is to cut a fire line and walk at a steady pace at the same time for as long as needed, sometimes for up to twelve hours. Once the fire is contained, we go into the burned areas and put out individual hot spots by scraping the burning coals from the trees or shoveling dirt on the flames or just digging smaller fire lines and letting the fire burn itself out. Then, when the fire's under control, we let the locals mop up what's left and head back to McCall.

Except this time we're the locals. The Payette is our National Forest, and after we contain the blaze, I volunteer to stay behind with Tex, Birddog, and Mike for two or three days to make sure we didn't miss any remaining fire.

So we have two or three days to hike up and down the hills looking for smoke, swim in the chilly waters of the Salmon River, have Pulaski-throwing contests, play poker around a campfire, and hunt rattlesnakes. These rocks and ravines are home to all kinds of snakes who like to come out in the afternoon and sun themselves, and I want to catch a rattler.

Even though this is my second summer on the job, I've never run into one. Part of our training has been to learn what to do if bitten, and I have a snakebite kit in my backpack, but so far, all I've seen are bull snakes, which look like the Northern Pacific rattlesnakes that live here but don't have the rattles.

Then, on the ground ahead of me in front of an opening in some rocks, I see a snake. I inch my way closer, but I still can't tell what kind it is. In addition to having rattles, rattlesnakes' eyes are more like cat's eyes than those on a bull snake, but I'm not near enough yet to tell.

When I'm maybe a couple of yards away, my foot crunches some gravel. Within seconds, the snake coils, raising its arrow-shaped head and tail. I hear the rattling. Without thinking, I take a giant step forward, swing my Pulaski over my head and drive it down through the snake, slicing it into three pieces.

The smallest piece is the head. I poke it with the Pulaski, noting its long thin tongue outside its mouth. I take the other two pieces to camp. Tex shows me how to skin them and hang the skins up on a branch to dry in tomorrow's sun. That night we have a rattlesnake appetizer (and yes, it tastes like chicken) to go with our canned Vienna sausages. Two days later, I take the largest skin, about fifteen inches long, with me.

The Geriatric Pilgrim

I know my life is transient, "like grass," as the psalmist says. Which is why I need to spend what's left of it looking at more than the small grove of fir trees out my back window. Especially in this time of not being able to travel physically, I need a wider view. Of ten-thousand-foot mountains and a river full of trout, salmon, mountain white fish, smallmouth bass, squawfish, and sturgeon. Of guys from California, Oregon, Washington, Utah, Texas, Oklahoma, Nebraska, Utah, and Colorado, with names like Bo Diddley, Birddog, Tex, Spankie, and Alfalfa.

A view that encompasses not only space but time: when I had a different name, "Froggie," because of the way I hopped when I was first learning to dig a fire line; when I could dig that fire line for twelve hours and then walk another ten miles out to a cattle truck taking me to the airport; when I could flip a Pulaski fifteen feet and stick it into a pine tree. When the stars at night seemed to be so close that I could reach out and grab one any time I wanted.

I doubt if I ever make a physical pilgrimage back to Idaho, where my vision of myself and my place in the world was transformed, but I can re-member that vision—that vitality and enthusiasm—simply by holding a dried-up snakeskin in my arthritic hands, and stand once more on one of those ten-thousand-foot mountains, gazing over the vast landscape of memory.

The Climbing Tree

When I was a kid, one of my favorite places in the world was at the top of a pine tree on the edge of the field behind our house. This tree was probably pretty small, but in my memory it loomed over me. I remember the first time I made it to the top, I felt as if my head were in the clouds. At the top of the tree, I found where a couple of branches had made a saddle, and from then on, I'd climb up, wedge myself into the branches, lean back, and watch those clouds. Sometimes they were dragons for me to conquer, sometimes ships to sail, sometimes castles where a great king lived. Sometimes the wind blew, rocking me back and forth. Usually, I could hear the river at the foot of the hill. As I grew older, I'd wonder who or what made these clouds and the wind and the river, which led to curiosity about who or what made me.

I thought of "my tree," the other day as I stood at the foot of a tall (and this one *is* tall) pine tree in the woods near our house, looking up at my eight-year-old grandson climbing from branch to branch. But while part of me was filled with nostalgia, part of me was scared to death. What if he slipped? My God, he might impale himself on that sharp limb below him. Oh, shit! Is that next branch safe?

Well, he didn't try to make it to the top, and he came down safely, and I didn't say anything, and we were both happy, but on the way home I got to thinking about how fearful I've become these days.

I don't like it.

The Geriatric Pilgrim

These fears probably began with Laurie's death thirty-two years ago—at least, that's when death for me became a reality instead of a concept. But it wasn't until twenty years later that the deaths of other people I knew and liked and loved started falling on me: first, as an occasional raindrop, now as steady precipitation—my classmates Marty and Tom, Laurie's mother, my wife's parents, my mother, more and more classmates like Roger and Scott, Diane and Audrey, my mentors and friends Mike and Andy. Then, two years ago, I, whose cholesterol levels, heart rate, and weight were all great, needed bypass surgery. Three months later, my former brother-in-law, who walked, swam, played tennis, and lifted weights suddenly dropped dead of the same kind of heart blockage that I'd had.

Not only did my surgery and Tom's death make death real, they made death something over which I—always a control freak—have no power over. And that's probably what really frightens me.

I realize the first things I think about when I wake up in the morning are all the bad stuff that might happen today to me or to someone I love. Will that ache in my shoulder turn out to be a heart attack? My wife's getting these serious pains in her knee. What if she has Parkinson's or becomes wheelchair bound? The wind's blowing again—what happens if that tree in the back yard falls on the house and kills Mary Lee or me? I can't find my keys again. Does that mean Alzheimer's?

Now, so far none of this has happened. My life is good. I often go to bed at night grateful for the day. Why can't I wake up in the morning in the same frame of mind?

I suspect I'm still fighting being mortal, still trying to hike mountains, lift rocks, throw a baseball, grasp new ideas the way I used to. I need to be spending a little more time with the Serenity Prayer: "God grant me the serenity to accept the things I cannot change, the courage to change the things I can, and the wisdom to know the difference."

So then, what can I change? What do I have control over?

I do have some control over how I die: my state has a "death with dignity" law. But at this point, I'm more interested in how I live until that time, and I don't want to spend my remaining days awfulizing about all the nasty things that could happen in between.

Maybe what I need to be asking myself, as time grows short and I age and break down, is what's most important to me? What do I want to be able to do for as long as possible?

Well, one of the things that's important to me is to be able to look at life the same way I did when I used to climb my pine tree. I had a destination. I looked up instead of down. I didn't mind if I got splinters or a little pitch on my hands. And once I'd gone as far as I could, I used my imagination and surrendered to the wonders of the natural world.

Okay, I can't go as far as I could, even a year ago. (Have I told you about my heel spur?) But I can still have a destination (a word, remember, that means purpose as well as place)—an essay or poem to write, a book to read—even if, like Stephen Hawking, I might have to write on a computer by twitching my cheeks, or "read" an audiobook. I won't mind a little pain or not looking young anymore as long as I can still be as curious about the changes in my grandchildren as I was about the changing shapes of the clouds. I can still find beauty and wonder in the outdoors, even if I might someday have to ask someone to wheel me outside to experience it.

That's all worth looking forward to. Worth living for.

I think it's time to stop asking myself in the morning, "What can go wrong today?" and start asking, "What is my destination today? What can I be curious about? Wonder at?"

A Pilgrim's Journal: August 2019

If you want to make God laugh, tell him about your plans.
—Woody Allen

IN TRYING TO CLEAN UP A BIT AFTER WHAT'S BEEN AN INTERESTING, to say the least, month, I found the guide for the cruise Mary Lee and I had booked for this summer. Turns out I took a cruise through heart surgery instead.

Thursday, July 18, 2019: Transfer from Oslo, Norway Airport to Hotel Bristol, Oslo. Oslo is…a medieval and Renaissance gem….

Thursday, July 18, 2019: Drive into Portland as the moon sets over Maine Medical Center. Check in, get a body shave, talk with my anesthesiologist, and then lose consciousness until I feel my esophagus being ripped out. Mary Lee, who's been waiting for me to come to, tells me the breathing tube has just been removed.

Friday, July 19 & Saturday, July 20: See gargantuan snowcapped mountains, magnificent fjords, and one of Europe's largest glaciers, as you travel to picturesque Bergen, an ancient city with deep Viking roots.

Friday, July 19: ICU, Maine Medical Center. Awake and panicky. Having trouble breathing. To prevent pneumonia, my nurse gets me up at three in the morning to sit in a chair until five thirty, when I go back to bed. Visit from P. from my 12-step program who works here. After someone tears drainage tubes out of my gut, I move from ICU to picturesque Room 104. Find the classical channel on TV and leave it on all night.

Saturday, July 20: Never could sleep on my back, just some drug induced Never Never Land. Wake around three with a medicinal smell in my nose and a clattering of trumpets from the TV that sounds like a party of drunken horses. Spend the day getting to know my nurse as she escorts me between bed, chair, and bathroom. Decide to write a country & western song, "Lasix and Me." Apparently, I've added ten pounds of fluid in my legs. Using a walker, I head down the hall with the nurse beside me and Mary Lee behind me with a wheelchair, which is good because I have to sit down after about sixty feet. Get my own incentive spirometer. Can barely bring it to 500 mg.

Sunday, July 21: Bergen, Norway. Enjoy a relaxing tour by deluxe motor coach as you tour the main sites…hear interesting stories about Bergen's colorful past.…

Sunday, July 21: Nice visit from my colorful rector, who's supposed to be on vacation, and B. from the men's group, who's full of interesting stories. Walk without a walker farther down the hall and back, but still must rest in the wheelchair halfway through. Spirometer up to 750 mg. Down two pounds of fluid.

Monday, July 22: Cruise to Geirangerfjord…Seven Sisters Waterfall… the Suitor Waterfall…Eagles Bend towers.…

Monday, July 22: Cruise down the hall to 111A, where I now share a room with J. When he orders a lobster roll and french fries for lunch, I almost throw up. Since Thursday, I've choked down a bowl of cereal, a fruit cup, and a container of yogurt. No waterfalls, but I do have my first shower. Make it around the nurses' station w/o walker or wheelchair and get the spirometer up to 1000 mg. Nice visits from friends and clergy. My nurse tells me I should go home tomorrow.

Tuesday, July 23: At Sea: Relax, Renew, Recharge at The Spa…peruse our Library.…

Tuesday, July 23: Maine Med. & Home. Still not sleeping, so I'm awake when they come to give me a chest x-ray at five fifteen. Get word I have a "slightly collapsed" left lung, so go for another x-ray at noon, then wait twenty minutes in what feels like a refrigerated meat locker for transport back to my room. Take another shower to warm up. Finally get word that the second x-ray shows no change and that my surgeon isn't worried. I can go home. Which means another two hours of paperwork plus getting rid of all the rest of the IV portals and wires. See myself. My chest looks like a zippered pincushion.

Home! Feel as if I've gone fifteen rounds with a black rhino.

Wednesday, July 24: Travel among the majestic mountains and fishing villages of the beautiful Lofoten Islands....

Wednesday, July 24: Two hours with R. from home health care. Two concerns: my back, which looks like I might be developing sores that can lead to infection, and my lungs, neither of which seems to be operating at anywhere near capacity. Try to do three ten-minute walks around beautiful Willow Grove. On a nice note (pun intended), receive more personal mail today than I've had in the last six years.

Thursday, July 25: Tromsø, Norway. Meet your local guide and drive through the city known as the Gateway to the Arctic....

Thursday, July 25: Don't quite make a mile around Willow Grove, but following the advice of Dr. R.'s nurse to put a pillow under my arm, I'm able to sleep on my side and, as a result, get the best night's sleep I've had in over a week. Feeling more improvement. After watching me climb stairs, get in and out of bed, and get up and down from the toilet, PT person from home health services says I don't need her.

Friday, July 26: Honningsvag, Norway. Take in...one of Europe's most stunning natural sights...the cliffs of Nordkapp rise more than one thousand feet from the sea waters and are topped by a large, flat plateau....

Friday, July 26: So much for stunning self-confidence: Today's nurse, J., is concerned about possible infection in the incisions made in my legs to get the vein for part of the bypass, so I'm blaming myself for not paying more attention to these incisions and for wearing the same pair of pants for three days. Now, these incisions seem to burn, and my face feels hot. Convinced I have a fever.

A Pilgrim's Journal: August 2019

Saturday, July 27 & Sunday, July 28: At sea. Designed in the spirit of the boutiques along the world's finest boulevards, we are proud to feature our onboard shops...clothing and handicrafts...jewelry and...cosmetics and skincare products.

Saturday, July 27: a night of catastrophizing. When I went to bed, my feet felt hot and tingly, and within fifteen minutes I'd developed kidney failure, started dialysis, and died. Tried Thich Nhat Hahn breathing exercises, prayers, Psalms, replaying the 1961 Class L State Basketball championship game. This morning after two phone calls, one to home health, and one to the surgeon's office, I'm told my options are to ride it out or go to the emergency room. Decide to ride it out. Walk up to the community garden (Mary Lee gives me a ride back.) Something cheerful about gardens.

Sunday, July 28: Best night's sleep so far. Increase my walking to fifteen minutes each time. Feet feel fine, but because I've got to have something to fret about, I'm concerned about my faster heart rate.

Monday, July 29: Shetland Islands....Farmland and dreamy meadows unfold toward seal-dotted beaches. Columnar sea stacks and rocky cliffs... medieval castles...Shetland ponies....

Monday, July 29: I've had three major operations and *The Lord of the Rings* has pulled me through each time. More aware this reading of the beauty of the language and the underlying sadness that runs through the entire trilogy. Even if the Ring-Bearer is successful against Evil, the world the characters know will fade away. Realize that despite priding myself on my ability to keep growing, keep changing, my life as I know it is slipping away—culturally, politically, physically—and today I want to cry.

Tuesday, July 30: Orkney Islands...embark on a scenic drive to the Ring of Brodgar, the finest known circular stone ring from the early Bronze Age...follow the coastline of Scapa Flow....

Tuesday, July 30: My sister brings over lobster rolls for lunch, as well as the obituary for my great-grandfather Bennett. Ever since I got the diagnosis of a blocked artery, I've been asking, Why me? My cholesterol levels have been low, as have blood pressure and heart rate. I've always been a walker and watch my weight and what I eat. Turns out, you can't fight your DNA. Grampy Bennett's obit reads like an autopsy: "At 6:00 p.m. last Saturday night, Clifford Bennett, age 63, died suddenly in his kitchen of acute indigestion. He'd been in good health prior." Googling "acute indigestion," I find that up until the 1920s that was the term for what we now know were heart attacks, often brought on by the same blocked main artery that I had.

Wednesday, July 31. Edinburgh, United Kingdom. See highlights of Scotland's capital city…from gracious architecture to a storied castle….

Wednesday, July 31. Our gracious friends J. & D., bring over supper for tonight: a shrimp and rice casserole with coleslaw. J's had a stroke, a bypass, and a valve replacement, and has just taken up rollerblading again. While I'm inspired enough to try walking without either my hiking poles or a walking stick, I'm not about to get on any damned roller skates, thank you very much.

Thursday, August 1: At Sea. We invite you to browse our selections of cutting-edge activewear at our onboard shop.

Thursday, August 1: Nice evening walk to water the garden, but then noticed before going to bed that my left ankle was swollen again. Spent the night browsing "The Catalogue of Really Horrible, Awful Things that Might Happen to Me." Finally took Tylenol and slept until almost eight o'clock. Called my 12-step sponsor and feel better.

Friday, August 2 & Saturday, August 3: London. Discover Greenwich's maritime and royal history by foot…Shakespeare's Globe Theater…West End musicals…Tower Bridge…the London Eye. Return home.

Friday, August 2: Mary Lee is off with one of the grandchildren, so I get up, meditate, go for a walk, fix and eat breakfast by myself—a first! Home health nurse says I'm doing well. Still some "crackling" in my lung and some swelling in my ankle, but I'm walking faster and standing straighter. Can keep the spirometer's button in the smiley face area for over five seconds each time.

Saturday, August 3: the day we should have been flying home, ending our original cruise. For this cruise through heart surgery, I've still got at least another month. I don't know what I'd have learned from those majestic mountains and castles and villages, but I have definitely learned at least two things on this trip. First, I'm not in control. Three months ago, I had no idea I had anything wrong with my heart. Now, I don't seem to have any command over how I'm doing each day, either physically or emotionally; all I can do is surrender my life to God of My Not Understanding.

Second, I live primarily through grace, in this case, the compassionate professionalism of my doctors and nurses, the cards and visits and emails from friends, and the unwavering love and support of my family, especially Mary Lee.

Not to mention the grace to have accepted my surgeon's advice and not put all this off until the middle of August.

Confessions of an Introvert

At some point during this pandemic, as COVID was winding down, I said at the men's group I help facilitate on Zoom that I was thankful for being an introvert. Except for not being able to be with my grandchildren, I said, my life hadn't changed all that much over the previous year: I wrote in the morning, I walked in the afternoon. I noodled on my banjo, read, and watched old movies on TV. Now, however, I admitted I was struggling to reenter society. The pace of life had picked up, the world seemed louder, and I had difficulty talking with people face to face.

"You're an introvert?" said a guy I've known for almost twenty years. "I'd never have known that."

Which surprised me at first, until I realized how often in my life I've tried to cover up my need for solitude, my dislike of large groups, and my discomfort around loud people because of feeling there is something wrong with me.

* * *

One of my earliest memories is of crawling into a cupboard next to the chimney in our living room and curling up in the dark next to the warm bricks. As I've written about earlier, I used to spend a lot of time as a boy nestled in my favorite pine tree watching the clouds. On weekends and when I was sick, I loved to curl up under the covers of my bed and listen to *Bobby Benson of the B-Bar-B*, *Sky King*, *Sergeant Preston of the Yukon*, and any number of other radio shows.

All that changed when I moved from the two-room primary school just up the street to the third grade in adjoining elementary and junior high schools. All at once, I was thrust into an intimidating world of sixth, seventh, and eighth graders, and because in those days, students routinely repeated grades, some of these kids were fifteen and sixteen years old. Bullying was common. I started waking up early in the morning fearful that Freddy Fitts would twist my arm behind my back and make me cry, the way he had with my classmate Roland.

That's when I discovered the value of safety in numbers. I joined a gang of guys who used to go around picking on solitary kids. It was mostly verbal (which still doesn't make me feel any better about some of the things I used to say), and I discovered I had a knack for the quick cutting remark. (See previous parenthetical comment.) Instead of a twisted arm, I got laughs.

When I began playing sports, I hung around with teammates, which fed my ego because athletes were looked up to. In high school, there were always friends at my house, a party or a dance every weekend, and joyriding around town in between. I was selected as "Class Wit."

Still, I occasionally snuck off by myself, sat by the river at the foot of the hill where I lived, and listened to the water and watched the birds. It's interesting to me that looking back sixty-plus years, I remember those times by the river more clearly than I remember parties I went to or dances I attended.

It was in college that I reverted to my introverted self, not because I wanted to, but because I never had the knack (and still don't, I'm finding on the rare occasions I go back into the world) of meeting new people. While my old high school classmates were joining fraternities, I sat in my dormitory room feeling as if the door were locked from the outside, convinced I was a failure for not being outgoing and popular.

After college, I found the perfect place to retreat into myself: on stage. (I'm not alone; I've read about countless actors, singers, and comedians who are deeply introverted.) My stage was my classroom, where I dressed in flashy sport coats, bell-bottomed trousers, bright matching ties and pocket handkerchiefs. I arranged the chairs so I was center stage. All to project confidence and wisdom. Every teaching day was like disappearing into an Iron Man suit. I felt invincible.

Until one day, I found Iron Man's hands around my neck, twisting the life out of me.

I left my job, my wife, my daughter, my house. I remarried, this time to a woman who loves what she calls "silence and slow time." Together, we began to practice meditation. (I remember that the first time I tried to meditate, I felt foolish. I imagined old high school classmates and my students calling me crazy, until I realized, no, I've been doing this all my life.) Mary Lee and I started going on silent retreats, making pilgrimages, or just traveling. Almost always alone, seldom on tours, avoiding for the most part the usual tourist spots.

* * *

Last week, I was telling another introvert about how often—and apparently successfully—I've hidden my introversion, and she recommended the book *Quiet: The Power of Introverts in a World That Can't Stop Talking* by Susan Cain. I'm fascinated, and somewhat relieved, by the way the author shows how this country changed its nineteenth-century emphasis on "character" to—thanks in large part to Dale Carnegie's book *How to Win Friends and Influence People*—a twentieth-century obsession with "personality," to the point where shy children have been stigmatized, even given drugs to make them more outgoing.

I imagine some of you reading this know better than I how difficult it can be to grow up as an introvert. How people often equate being shy with being weak. I remember a principal I worked for who wrote in his evaluation that I was *diffident*, a word I had to look up. When I found it meant "lacking confidence, timid, shy," I challenged him. Come to find out, he wasn't talking about my classroom teaching, he was talking about the way I'd chaired a faculty meeting on accreditation, something I'd never in my life done before. (My next principal, by the way, at my going away party when I left the school, called me "one of our towering presences.")

So how will any of this help me resurface after these years of "silence and slow time," especially into a world that has grown louder and more aggressive? Well, even as I was writing the last paragraph, I realized that there's still part of me that believes introverted means weak and that I need to hide behind some kind of extroverted persona. One of my temptations in this book, for example, has been to pose as more of a world traveler than I am. (I've lived all but four years of my life in one state, for heaven's sake!)

Enough people have told me I'm a good teacher that I believe them, but if so, I continued to be a good teacher after I stopped wearing the matching neckties and pocket handkerchiefs. I didn't need to pose. I just enjoyed teaching. And I don't need to pose as a wandering adventurer to approach the world with the curiosity and wonder of a pilgrim. I can accept, even relish, being an introvert and try to maintain the more leisurely pace of the last years, no matter what the rest of the world is doing, making time for plenty of solitude with God of My Not Understanding. I can become more involved in my Al Anon and Adult Children of Alcoholics groups, made up predominantly of fellow introverts (which makes me wonder how much of being an introvert is nature and how much is nurture or the lack thereof).

And I can still call this book *The Geriatric Pilgrim*.

Up to the Garden

ONCE OR TWICE A DAY FROM MAY TO OCTOBER, I'LL MAKE A SHORT pilgrimage (it takes six minutes) to our community garden (or as we say in Maine, "gahden"). At my little plot, which is about the size of our dining room table, I'll examine my half-row of peas, two kale plants, two broccoli plants, one pole of beans, and six tomato plants. I may pull a few weeds. If it's been dry, I'll water from the community hose system. Then I'll return home, strangely refreshed, more at peace with the world.

I need to be honest here: I'm not a real "gahdnah." I know many people who have an abiding passion for gardening, while over the years, my interest in growing flowers and vegetables has waxed and waned.

Which makes me wonder why tending a few vegetables is so soothing to my soul these days. What do my on-and-off bouts of gardening tell me about the longer pilgrimage I'm on, the landscape through which I'm traveling?

* * *

From age thirteen to seventeen, I worked in a local market garden. Willian Bryant Logan writes in his fascinating book *Dirt: The Ecstatic Skin of the Earth*: "Work, motion, life. All rise from the dirt and stand upon it as on a launching pad." I certainly rose from that garden dirt. At thirteen, I was five feet nine inches, and at seventeen, I was six foot two. But that was only part of the growth. I worked with a bunch of other high school students, guys and gals. We guys spent our lunch hours and after work playing basketball; thus, the garden was my basketball summer camp. The guys and gals flirted and sometimes dated (and two of my former coworkers have now been married over fifty years), making the garden a school for sex education. I learned to drive a tractor, so the garden was my driver's ed. Besides sports, we also talked about politics (we were all John Kennedy fans), and so the garden introduced me to a world outside of Maine.

And I sure as hell learned how to work. I learned how to work eight to ten hours a day seven days a week. I learned how to work with next to no sleep. I learned how to work hungover. Some of us from those years remain in contact, and I'm interested that even though we're all dancing around eighty, we're all still working at one kind of job or another.

* * *

For fifteen years, I had a big garden—around five acres as I recall—in Down East Maine. I raised enough vegetables to feed three families: mine, my in-laws, and my wife's aunt and her son. From March to November, I spent every spare moment in that garden. I loved it. If you asked me why, I'd have said it was because I was getting fresh air and exercise, I was helping us eat healthy, and because I could peer across the road at the ocean, or look up and see an occasional eagle, or gaze into the woods and often see deer or fox.

But the real reason I loved working in that garden is because it helped me live in a failing marriage. For sometimes eight hours a day I could escape the passive-aggressive bickering and then plead exhaustion so I could avoid it further by going to bed. The garden was where I could fantasize about writing the Great American Novel, becoming famous, or seducing beautiful women. But the garden was also a place of healing where, before I understood the importance of meditation, I would lose myself in the moment. (My former father-in-law used to say that I spent five minutes working and two minutes staring off into space.) The garden was where I could be in control—planning, planting, tending, harvesting, and putting everything to bed—where I could measure success and failure by the baskets of potatoes or sacks of peas and beans I harvested.

After the divorce court pronounced the marriage legally dead, however, my thoughts about gardening were tied in with failure and anger. For the next thirty years, I was very content to get my summer vegetables at the farmers' market.

* * *

So what's happened? Why am I once more playing in the dirt, even on such a small scale? And even more intriguing, why—despite last year's cutworms killing two tomato plants and five bean plants, rabbits nibbling my peas, and the peas themselves deciding to climb into the tomato cages instead of up the trellis I made for them—am I, as of this writing, eagerly planning next year's garden?

I think because, as in those years of living in a lousy marriage, I'm in need of escape and healing. This is another lousy time. There's coronavirus in the air, protests in the streets, a dictator attacking Europe, and dangers to our democracy at home. In addition to once again helping me live in the moment, dirt and mud are themselves natural antidepressants; apparently, the bacteria found in them trigger the release of serotonin in our brains. Dirt is the source of the greater part of our drugs against infectious diseases. Dirt neutralizes poisons, and I'm wondering if besides poisons in the ground, dirt doesn't help neutralize the toxic atmosphere of today's political climate. (Not to mention what's happening to our natural environment.)

Gardening teaches me that no matter how old or feeble I feel, I can still bring about new growth, still contribute, and still learn—perhaps not as exuberantly as when I was sixteen, but more wisely with the benefit of another sixty years of experience. My little garden is almost entirely compost, made of what I and my neighbors contribute year-round from what I used to think of as waste. Compost tells me that in nature, there's no such thing as waste. I read somewhere that we ourselves are compost, composed of dust from stars that have died. Compost, then, is a lot like resurrection: life's dregs—death, if you will—transformed into the basis of new life.

And since I'm being quasi-religious, gardening is a lesson in grace. I can prepare the ground, I can water, I can put collars around my tomato plants to stop the cutworms, but without the help of sun and rain and the right temperatures—all of which are beyond my control—nothing will grow.

Above all, gardening is an act of hope, something I for one desperately need these days. It's a bet on the future. Not only on this country's or this world's future, but on my own possibilities for productivity. (Last year, I had pole beans still blossoming well into September.)

There was a popular singing group in the 1950s called the Weavers, whose music I still enjoy. (They popularized the song, "Goodnight Irene.") Lee Hayes, who, besides singing bass in the quartet, was an avid gardener, stipulated in his will that his ashes be mixed into his compost pile.

I'm committed to my family cemetery, but I understand the impulse.

Showing Up

A friend—I'll call him Gary—has neighbors whose twenty-year-old son recently died in an automobile accident. Because Gary knows I've lost a child, he asked me if I had any advice on what he could say to them. Although I shy away from giving anyone advice on grieving (more on that later), I did send him some thoughts about what helped me and what made things worse in the years immediately after Laurie died. A month or so later, he wrote to thank me because what I'd written was showing him how to be with his neighbors in ways they seemed to appreciate.

Because it appears to have helped Gary, and because, as I write this, over a million people in this country have died from COVID, and innocent men, women, and children are dying in Ukraine, I'm going to pass on what I emailed Gary for any of you who know someone who, while they may not have lost a child, is in grief this year.

* * *

My experience and reading both say that it's not what you *should* say to parents when a child dies, but what you *shouldn't* say. Even the most well-meant words can ignite anger and shame. For example:

- "*Let me know if there's anything I can do to help.*" The first time I heard someone say this to me after Laurie died, I thought,

Showing Up

Yeah, my life is a mountain of rubble and you want me to think of things for you to do? Well, screw you!

- *"How are you doing?"* How the hell did I know? My entire world—my values, my belief in God, my image of how the world works—had just been obliterated. Often, I would mumble, "Fine." Later, I joined a 12-step program and learned "fine" means "Fucked up, Insecure, Numb, and Empty." Which was about right.
- *"Be grateful for the time you had together."* This is like telling someone who's just had both of their legs blown off to be thankful they used to be able to walk.
- *"Everything happens for a reason."* This is another comment that still has me pounding the walls, along with, "God doesn't give you anything you can't handle," or "God must have wanted another angel in heaven." Well, if God is that kind of super sadist, you can send me to Hell.
- *"I know exactly how you feel."* Usually followed by, "When my grandfather/uncle/mother/ dog died…." I'm sorry, but if you really knew how I feel, you'd shut the hell up.
- *"Grief just takes time."* How the hell is that supposed to help me get through the day, let alone nights that are five years long?
- *"You need to get on with your life, get back to normal."* I first heard this a month after Laurie died. The most recent time was about a year ago. My response hasn't changed: This *is* my life. There will never be anymore goddamned "normal."
- *"At least she's no longer suffering."* Or *"She's at peace."* And I'm still grieving like hell, thank you very much.

It's not that some of these are necessarily bad advice. Thirty years after Laurie's death, I am happy for the time we had together. The effects of grief do lessen over time. I do think she's in a better place. I have moved on, and while my life has never returned to "normal," it is in some ways happier. One of the ironies of suffering—at least for me—is that in breaking me open, it also opened this introverted New England male to joy.

But when I'm grieving I don't want advice, even the most well-intentioned. In my shame and my anger, your advice makes me feel that you're on some pedestal of knowledge looking down on me, and I'm just that much more isolated in my pain.

What I need is to feel is that you're beside me.

* * *

So, is there anything you can say?

Not much. Maybe something along the lines of *"I'm thinking of you and wish there were words to comfort you."* I did find it helpful to have people ask me what happened, and more helpful if someone asked me about Laurie in ways that I could talk about what a beautiful, compassionate kid she was. I was particularly grateful if someone who had known my daughter had a story to share with me about her. I appreciated flowers and cards and the donations made in Laurie's name, not only to the Cancer Society and the Ronald McDonald House, but also to Pilgrim Lodge Summer Camp and Amnesty International, two of Laurie's favorite organizations.

Some writers about grief suggest providing information on grief counselors or helping parents plan some kind of memorial. Although I later sought counseling and bought a memorial stone for my daughter to place in our family cemetery, I didn't want any of that at first. For over a year after Laurie's death, I just wanted to be left alone. But at the same time, I wanted to know someone was there when I needed them.

Bottom line: it's a question of doing, not saying. What can you do for the grieving parent—cards, flowers, meals? Can you give them a call every week or so simply to say, "How about those Red Sox?"

It's especially important not to disappear after the first month or so. That's just another way of saying "You need to get on with your life."

Let people grieve. Listen. Don't judge. I met with a woman for almost a year after her son died—gave her all kinds of advice, books to read. A few years later, I ran into her and she said how much I'd helped her.

"Anything I said in particular?" I said, looking for guidance on what to say to others.

"I don't remember a damn thing you said," she told me. "All I remember is that you cared enough to have lunch with me once a week."

So, I try never to give advice to anyone who's grieving unless they ask for it. I'm also leery enough about giving advice to people who want to help someone in grief to caution that everyone grieves differently and, as a rule, men and women grieve differently (which contributes to the higher-than-average divorce rate among grieving parents.)

But if I were to give you any advice, I'd simply say, *Shut up and show up.*

Putting Away the Past

On January 7, the day after we Episcopalians celebrate Epiphany, I put on music from *The Christmas Revels* (a compact disc; we wore out the tape we bought right after we'd seen a performance of this Solstice celebration over thirty years ago) and begin to take down our Christmas tree, removing the ornaments, packing them away for another year.

We take off the unbreakable ornaments first. Most of them come from our travels: several woolen sheep of various sizes and a wooden long-haired highland cow from Scotland, probably our favorite country to visit; a couple of olivewood Jerusalem crosses from Israel; a weighty wooden St. Nicholas from Cambridge, England; and a porcelain *nazar*, an eye-shaped Turkish amulet believed to protect against the evil eye, which we bought in the Grand Bazaar in Istanbul.

Putting them away in the bottom of the box, I think of Columba's Bay on Iona, the cobweb of streets in the Old City of Jerusalem, drinking Green King Ale in The Champion on the Thames with Dick and Janet Graham, and sharing Turkish meze platters with our friends Lynne and Finlay. Later today, I might dig out a map or a travel guide to expand a snippet of memory into a full narrative, some of which might actually have happened. If not, so what? It's my memory.

Next, we take off the homemade ornaments from the children and grandchildren. Mary Lee's sons used to make God's eyes—you

Putting Away the Past

know, running different colored yarn around various sized crosses. We've also got decorations showing the boys' growth into adulthood: a couple of felt cats named for Jeremy's first two pets that followed him around from one apartment to another, and—perhaps our most unique ornament—a soft brown diarrhea microbe, which was from Jeremy's wedding to a professor whose PhD is in Tropical and Diarrheal Diseases.

Our most recent additions to the tree are from last year, when all four grandchildren were into fuse-beads, which for those of you who haven't played with grandchildren lately are colorful beads arranged on a plastic pegboard to form a pattern or a shape and then fused together with a clothes iron (which is, quite frankly, the only time we've used an iron in the last twenty years).

Many of the more fragile ornaments come from our childhoods and get wrapped in tissue paper. Mary Lee has an angel that her mother remembered from when she was a girl, making it around a hundred years old. I've got a couple of glass ornaments from our family tree, as well as a plastic Santa Claus on skis from the 1940s that I'm pretty sure came with a six-pack of Coca-Cola, which I used to drink in vanilla ice cream floats on Christmas Day after we'd opened our presents (which would have been about nine in the morning. Yeech!).

Perhaps because my parents grew up in homes where Christmas was fraught with alcoholism and other family dysfunction, they tried hard to make sure their children's Christmases were happy ones. And on the whole, they succeeded. For me, Christmas is a time to remember and honor my family, not just my parents and siblings, but the extended family of which I am a part.

The two ornaments Mary Lee gave me for our first Christmas together go in their own boxes: a red ball—naturally—for the Boston Red Sox and a silver-and-green one for the Boston Celtics. Both teams have had their ups and down over the last thirty-five years, but by and large, they've done well. Mary Lee and I have also had our ups and downs, but I think we've done even better.

My most prized ornament, and I usually pack it away last so that it's right on top to put on first next year, is a cloth ornament my daughter embroidered for Mary Lee and me for our first Christmas together. Laurie was sixteen at the time, two years away from the cancer that killed her. Wrapping the ornament, I see by her signature on the back that this was the year she called herself by her middle name, "Leigh." A time when a future of limitless possibility seemed to lie before her.

It usually takes just about as long to put away the ornaments as it does to listen to the entire *Christmas Revels*, which I'll also set aside for another year. These songs and dances celebrate the fusion of Christianity and the pagan festivals surrounding the winter solstice and the rebirth of the year. In many ways, they are a dance of light and dark, death and life, past and present.

I'm packing away, then, not only ornaments but memories and stories, both happy and sorrowful. And while I think it's important, especially as I age, not to dwell on the past but to focus on the present and the future, these ornaments will stay with me throughout the rest of the year in some closet of my subconscious, subtle yet constant reminders that what has saved me before in times of grief, illness, and addiction—faith, family, friends, the natural world, art and music—can save me in the future.

Navigating the Death of an Ex

I HAVE BEEN WITH MY PARENTS DURING THEIR FINAL HOURS. I HAVE witnessed my daughter take her last tortured breaths. I am watching old friends die almost monthly. Still, I've never felt such a mix of emotions as I did when I stumbled across my ex-wife's obituary in the newspaper.

Happily remarried for thirty years, I'd had no contact with her since our daughter's death four years after the divorce. Since that time, I seldom thought of my first marriage except as a twenty-year mistake, most of the mistakes being hers.

But now I felt weak. I found myself thinking, *If only we'd stayed in our first house instead of moving back to her hometown, we might have made the marriage work. If only we'd seen a marriage counselor. If only I'd gone for a PhD and become a college professor instead of remaining a high school English teacher....*

Then I thought, *if my ex and I had stayed married, I wouldn't be with Mary Lee, who showed me what marriage can be, who was the reason I didn't drink myself to death when Laurie died, who makes me believe God really does exist. There's no way I could be happier than I am now.*

For weeks, I felt like a racquetball, caroming off walls of shock, relief, regret, and gratitude.

But there was no one to talk with about how I felt. No action I could take. When my mother and father died, my brother, sister, and I shared memories. We purchased another stone for the family cemetery to decorate on Memorial Day. After Laurie died, I found groups like Compassionate Friends with whom I could talk. I made contributions for cancer research. I counseled other grieving parents.

But I couldn't put a memorial stone for my ex-wife in our family lot. And while Mary Lee was sympathetic—she'd spent weeks listening to a friend describe her conflicted feelings after her ex died—I couldn't talk to her about the "if onlys" and the "what ifs" of my first marriage, the experiences only my ex and I shared, especially with our daughter. I was now the only one alive to remember Laurie's first steps as she stumbled between her mother and me, or my sitting with her mother during our daughter's first piano recital, or the three of us decorating the Christmas tree.

Add loneliness to the emotional cesspool in which I swam.

Then, during a meeting of the 12-step program to which I belong, when my emotions about my ex-wife's death were swarming like black flies, I shared that when I'd gone away to college, I anticipated getting away from my dysfunctional family, but that my mother's shame and my father's angry resentments had come with me. My grades were lousy. I was lonely, bitterly envious of the fraternity brothers and sorority sisters on campus, but resistant to making friends because anyone who'd be my friend would be a loser, just like me.

Driving home after the meeting, I realized how being a child of alcoholism had drawn me into marrying an only child from a close-knit family with firm Yankee values who seemed confident and strong, and who, I thought, would offer me the stability I craved.

I started to realize how being that child had also contributed to the breakup of the marriage. How, to keep feeling safe and secure, I never expressed any of my own needs. How I used sarcasm or said, "I'm sorry" without meaning it to avoid arguments. How I worked long hours at school to gain respect from my students and to avoid problems at home. How I built up resentments like building blocks until they finally came crashing down around my wife, my daughter, and me.

I found myself feeling not only more compassion for my ex, but also for the marriage itself. We did remain married for twenty years. At least ten of them were pretty good. Most importantly, we created an intelligent, beautiful, compassionate daughter, who, although she died at eighteen, continues to inspire me every day. There's no way in the world I could wish Laurie had never happened.

With the help of my 12-step sponsor, I began to see the best way—maybe the only way—for me to grieve my ex-wife's death was to honor the good times in our marriage. learn from the mistakes I made, and not repeat them.

I wrote a letter to my sarcasm, thanking him for helping me get through some ugly times, but saying his services were no longer needed and it was time for him to retire to a condo in Florida.

I worked to become more honest, more open in my relationships with others. Probably because of our struggles to understand each other after Laurie's death, Mary Lee and I had usually been able to speak openly with each other, but I made even more of an effort. With other people, I tried to listen more, wait (a 12-step acronym, by the way, for "Why Am I Talking?") before reacting, and, when I did respond, to focus on "I" statements—"I feel…" "I see it this way…"—rather than "you" statements—"You're wrong…" "You don't understand…" "You need to…" (This has also helped me talk with Mary Lee, come to think of it.)

Since the advent of COVID—and now with the events in Ukraine—I'm learning another lesson from my first marriage. I was drawn to my ex because she made me feel strong and secure. As she and I discovered, however, the world is not a safe place: I brought my dysfunctional family behavior into our marriage; both she and I underwent major surgeries; our daughter died of a rare cancer. Mary Lee and I are in our seventies, and although we're vaccinated and still mask, we're at risk. I've had more surgery; she's prone to pneumonia. I'm watching more and more friends die from other causes—cancer of the jaw, Parkinson's, heart disease—and I find myself wanting to hunker down, stay home, or perhaps sell our house and move into a continuing care facility as some other friends are doing because they feel they'll have more security.

But looking at the failure of my first marriage helps me see that real strength comes not from trying to avoid risk, but from living with curiosity, honesty, and love, both for my family and for myself.

Which is why at the beginning of last summer, Mary Lee and I found a window between the waves of pandemic to take a European cruise. I've called a contractor to do some remodeling of our house. We both volunteered to facilitate adult education programs.

And in the years to come? I can't know, of course. I expect that my family's history of heart disease and cancer will hunt me down. Grieving my ex-wife's death, however, has helped me see that I can't let the desire for stability dictate the way I live my life.

Been there. Done that. Didn't work.

A Pilgrim's Journal: July 2021

7/25: Amsterdam. We're here. Right up until the plane took off, I wasn't sure this trip would ever happen. Over the last two years, I've booked two cruises and canceled both, once because of my health and once because of the nation's. This spring, I had a painful bone spur in my heel. For the last week, I've been reading and worrying about flooding along the Rhine. And after over a year of staying at home, I find myself anxious and reluctant to travel to another state, let alone another continent.

On the plane from Boston, I started reading Sharon Salzburg's *Real Change*, in which she talked about our three responses to stress—flight, fight, and freeze—and I realized how frozen I've been during this pandemic.

This was painfully clear at Logan Airport. After waiting in line at the ticket counter, Mary Lee and I were told we needed to fill out a special COVID questionnaire to get into Ireland (never mind that we were only in Ireland to change planes), and that this form needed to be filled out on our iPhones. I literally froze. I couldn't get my fingers to work and had step out of line to have Mary Lee do the damn thing for me. By taking so long, we got stuck in the last two seats in the back of the plane, which meant being the last off the plane in Dublin, which meant running (or what passes for running at my age) from one end of the airport to the other, which meant barely making our connecting flight.

But after walking the streets of Amsterdam over the canals, I can feel myself thawing a bit, feel myself flowing with the pedestrians and bicyclists, past people relaxing in front of cafés and coffee shops.

7/26: We've started our cruise on the lower Rhine, where many trees and bushes along the banks are still under water after the floods. Still, I'm finding being on the river serene. I've always found rivers calming. I grew up by a river. I've often imagined my life as part of a river flowing from my forebears to an indeterminate future just around the next bend. This morning, Mary Lee and I meditated on our little balcony outside our stateroom, and I watched the Rhine through half-closed eyes and felt myself rocked. Held.

7/27: Cologne. Our excursion this morning was primarily through the fourteenth-century Gothic cathedral, one of the few buildings not destroyed in WWII by Allied planes. Supposedly, it holds the bones of the Magi and was a site for pilgrimages in the Middle Ages.

For me, however, it was finding the Kathe Kollwitz Museum during our free time this afternoon that was my pilgrimage. Kollwitz was an early twentieth-century German artist who worked with painting, printmaking, and sculpture. Reading her diaries after her son Peter had been killed in World War I, I saw how powerful art can be, not in eliminating but in transforming grief, and Kollwitz's seventeen-year long struggle to create a monument to her son inspired me to keep plugging away at my novel, *Requiem in Stones*, based on the death of my own child.

7/28: Koblenz: We're forty-five miles from Weilburg (pronounced, I find, "Vile-borg"), where my paternal ancestors originated before moving to Nova Scotia in 1750. No time to visit, but I've got it on my bucket list.

Koblenz, like Cologne, was 90 percent destroyed in WWII, so I didn't feel as if I were looking at the physical layering of history the way I did, let's say, in Turkey, where stones from churches, mosques, and palaces from one era were used in erecting new buildings. Instead, I felt as if I was viewing Germany's efforts to layer at another level its often problematic past into its contemporary consciousness. Today, for example, we saw copper inserts in the sidewalks in memory of local Jews who were killed during the war, as well as the History Column, a monument depicting two thousand years of city history in ten scenes from Roman times to today.

Then this afternoon, what's called the Middle Rhine carried us by sixteen or seventeen magnificent castles rising out of the mountains, and I had an out-of-body experience of floating through not only Germany's history, but mine, sensing the river that is my life extending back much further than I'd imagined, and flowing far further into the future.

7/29: Speyer. More history, courtesy of "Hermann, the German," our eighty-nine-year-old tour guide, who talked from personal experience about wartime Germany—of being a schoolboy wearing the Nazi brown shirt because if he hadn't, he wouldn't have been able to go past elementary school, and of his father, a German soldier who spent two years after the war in a French prison camp.

Appropriately, I thought, our walking tour ended at a statue of a Jakobspilger, or St. James's pilgrim. Speyer is part of the Camino de Santiago, the famous pilgrimage route to the Spanish town of Santiago de Compostela, where, according to Christian tradition, the Apostle Saint James was buried.

This trip is turning out to be far more of a pilgrimage than I'd thought it would be. Denial has been a big part of my life, especially my childhood. Seeing how Germans deal with their past, especially their Nazi past, will, I hope, help me be more aware, more honest about accepting my own history.

7/30: Strasbourg. Brief trip into France. The Cathedrale Notre-Dame de Strasbourg is another church that was at one time the highest building in Europe. The churches I've seen so far on this trip illustrate—at least to me—how religion always becomes politicized. These cathedrals may contain stained-glass pictures from the Bible, but I also saw statue after statue of some general or king in armor wielding a sword. After seeing these churches, I realize I shouldn't find the political agendas of fundamentalists unusual.

The Geriatric Pilgrim

Another lesson in acceptance, I suppose.

In our free time this afternoon, Mary Lee and I wandered beside the canals before eventually stopping in a square for hot chocolate (me), coffee (her), a croissant, and people watching. Scribbling in my notebook, I felt like Ernest Hemingway—probably my earliest creative influence—writing in Paris in the 1920s, and felt, as I always do when I think of Papa, rejuvenated.

7/31: Breisach and the Black Forest. More cruising into my past. Germany's Black Forest reminds me of Idaho's Payette Forest, where I worked for two summers, another invigorating time for me. Mary Lee and I joined a hike to a waterfall. I'm sure we were the oldest ones on that hike, and I was pleased we were able to keep up.

8/1: Basal, Switzerland. On the balcony outside our stateroom on the boat, waiting for the bus to Lucerne and the end of our trip, I read more of Sharon Salzburg's *Real Change*: "When I want to summon strength and power in the midst of awfulness and hate, I contemplate water. [Water is]…always changing, in motion, yet revealing continual patterns of behavior."

I've found these "continual patterns" fascinating on this trip, from my reintroduction to the serenity of rivers, to the renewal of my love of Kollwitz and Hemingway, to my continued love of forests and streams, to my feeling part of the river of Wiles flowing from Weilburg, Germany to and past the cemetery in Maine where my ashes will lie.

Salzburg also wrote that yes, water can freeze, but it can also thaw. And I feel thawed out. My challenge is to continue feeling this way.

This morning at breakfast, we looked across what is now the Upper Rhine to the other shore to see a naked man emerge from the river, where he'd been for a swim, and walk down a boardwalk to his clothes. Most people found the guy hilarious. I, however, saw him as an icon for starting each day rising from a river, naked, newly born.

Metaphorically speaking, of course. I don't even take my shirt off at the beach anymore.

Dancing Lessons

For many people like my parents, music and dancing are intertwined. But while I have always loved music—from the ragtime my grandmother played on our piano to my CDs of Elvis, Charlie Parker, Willie Nelson, Mozart, and the Carolina Chocolate Drops—I have not always loved dancing.

I blame Arthur Murray, who, it has been said, taught America to dance. In the 1950s, when I first discovered rock 'n roll and girls, there were over three thousand Arthur Murray dance studios in the United States, one of which sent instructors (I remember him as thirtyish, with thinning hair, wearing a wrinkled tuxedo, and her as blonde—bleached?—in a black strapless dress that showed off her legs and the run in her stocking) to Yarmouth, Maine, to line us boys up on one side of the room and the girls on the other, leaving a no-man's-land between the sexes that I spent years trying to cross.

Apparently, Murray, whose given name was Moses Teichman and who grew up on the Lower East Side of Manhattan, felt that dancing was how people could become more sophisticated and move, as he had, into a "better" class of society. Besides teaching the steps to the waltz, the foxtrot, the jitterbug, and the cha-cha, the instructors also taught etiquette. Young men were instructed to walk across the floor to the young ladies, bow, and say, "May I have this dance?"

I have to say, however, that if the aim was to teach refined behavior to seventh and eighth graders, it was not a good idea, after having taught us the steps, to blow a god damned whistle. The resulting melee resembled the kickoff of a football game, as barely pubertal males raced across the floor, elbowing each other in a furious attempt to get to the four or five girls with breasts, the fastest and dirtiest fighters skidding to a stop in front of them, yelling "My'vethisdance!" while the chosen ones stood giggling and the rest of the girls stared at the floor, waiting for the losers to get to them.

I learned to see dancing as a fight for survival of the fittest. And when I reached high school, the record hops in the gymnasium buttressed my understanding that dancing was a battle in which I first had to get up the nerve to cross the no-man's-land between the guys standing along one wall and gals standing along the other, get up the courage to look a girl in the eye, struggle to find something to say, wrestle with how close to get and where to put my hands, and finally retreat without feeling like a coward.

Until one night, I didn't retreat. We talked. We laughed. The music continued and dancing became unlike anything I'd ever experienced. Looking into her eyes, seeing both her and me for the first time, I surrendered my adolescent self-consciousness to an interplay of body, mind, and music.

Fast-forward twenty-five years. I'm in Princeton, New Jersey, evaluating high school essays for the College Board. The last night of the reading, a bunch of us teachers are in a bar, bouncing our middle-aged bones around the dance floor to a collection of golden oldies played by some kids in ripped T-shirts. When the band switches from "Whole Lotta Shakin' Going On," to "I Can't Help Falling in Love with You," the woman I've been twisting with says, "Do you dance slow?"

Nearly forty years later, we still try to get in at least one slow dance a week.

Dancing Lessons

* * *

Perhaps because writing these reflections has made me more aware of connections, I'm wondering if my relationship with God of My Not Understanding hasn't also been a kind of dancing lesson.

In the first years after Laurie died, any contact I had with God felt, first, like those early Arthur Murray days—trying to follow the directions of well-meaning instructors, navigate the frightening no-man's-land between God and me, while wrestling with anger, fear, and shame, and then—like the high school dances—getting up the nerve to ask God for help, struggling to find words to express my grief, even grappling with where to put my hands when I tried to pray.

And over thirty years after Laurie's death, I still sometimes feel like Jacob in the Old Testament, wrestling with, if not God, then with God's angel.

And yet gradually over the years, I have also often felt embraced, taken into loving arms in a dance to what I can only call the music of grace, grace not only to survive Laurie's death, but also to have lived a happy, often joy-filled, life. And I realize these are the times I've surrendered—let God lead, if you will—losing, and at the same time, finding myself in the embrace of a Higher Power.

Both scientists and modern writers on spirituality tell us everything in the universe—animals, vegetables, minerals, living and dead—is interconnected. Everything exists in relationship. The question for me these days (and I wonder if it isn't a question this country is struggling to answer), is whether the relationship is going to be in the form of a battle or a dance—whether when I look out my window at tree branches in the wind, I see the trees battling the elements or dancing to them; whether when I see someone of another color or another life-style coming toward me on the street, I see an opponent or a partner; whether I still see the world as us and them lined up on opposite sides of the floor, or whether I see just us, moving like Mary Lee and me on a date night in harmony to the music.

Where I Need to Be

As mentioned earlier in these pages, Mary Lee and I were twice forced to cancel a cruise up the Norwegian coast to the Arctic Circle and back along the coast of Scotland and England—once because I discovered I had a "moderately severe" blocked left main artery in my heart and once when COVID shut down the world.

I don't think we'll ever make this trip.

Yeah, I'm disappointed, but in looking back at other trips and pilgrimages I've made, I can see that there have been times when not going where I planned to go has given me what I've needed.

Maybe this is one of those times.

* * *

I'm thinking of the first day Mary Lee and I walked from our guest house in Jerusalem into the Old City. Our plan was to go to the Church of the Holy Sepulchre, the traditional site of Christ's crucifixion and burial. But do you think we could find it? We wandered narrow street after narrow street, fighting the heat, the souvenir sellers, the money changers, going, I later found out, in circles. I grew hot, tired, and frustrated, first with Mary Lee for wanting to come to Israel, then with God for making it so hot, and then, as long as I was blaming God for things, flashing back to those days when my daughter was dying and each day seemed a confusing maze through which I wandered, alone and lost.

Where I Need to Be

Suddenly, we were standing in what seemed like a big parking lot in front of the Western Wall, the most religious site in the world for Jewish people: huge blocks of cream-colored limestone called Jerusalem stone, the remnants of the old Jewish temple. At the base of the wall, dozens of men and women rocked and bobbed. I heard chanting. As if the wall were a magnet, I found myself pulled toward it. As I neared the wall, I noticed cracks and veins running through the stones, every cleft stuffed with prayers written on anything from Post-It Notes to legal stationery. I watched a man write on a piece of paper, fold it, and carefully tuck it into a fissure in the wall. He leaned forward and gently touched his lips to the stone. Although I hadn't planned to do so, I ripped a page out of my notebook, wrote a prayer for Laurie, and tucked it into one of the crevices. It was perhaps the most spiritual moment of the entire pilgrimage.

* * *

When Mary Lee and I were making plans to see the giant Redwoods in California, we intended to stay for a few days at the same European-style hotel in San Francisco that we'd been in a few years earlier, but it was full, so I chose what I thought was a comparable hotel. Nope, this one was rundown, dirty, and at night, a place where battalions of mosquitoes gathered for R&R.

What I hadn't known when I made the reservations was that this hotel was almost across the street from City Lights Book Store, a second home for writers of the Beat Generation. I was beginning to become active in Al Anon, and visiting City Lights, remembering Jack Kerouac, one of the towering figures of my youth, and rereading his books were what I needed to better understand the effects alcoholism has had on me.

* * *

I've just made a list of some of my other plans that haven't panned out: study forestry and become a district ranger somewhere in the

American West; earn a PhD in Maine Literature and become a professor at the University of Maine at Orono; buy a house on the coast of Down East, Maine and father two children; become chair of the English Department at a large high school in Southern Maine and, when I retire, become a consultant for the College Board; move back to my old hometown of Yarmouth and become a pillar of the community.

And yet, sitting here in Brunswick, Maine, I see that if these plans hadn't failed, my life would be the poorer. (Actually, I'm not sure I'd be alive.) Failing as a forester led me to the joy of literature at a time when I was lost and confused about who I was. Not becoming a college professor meant I could pass on what I'd learned about college expectations to high school students, feel the joy of watching a light bulb go off in a seventeen-year-old's head, and sense I'd made a difference in the world. A painful divorce led to love that I'd never thought possible. Early retirement from teaching meant that I've been able to devote myself to writing, which I've needed to do to offset living with the death of my daughter. Leaving my hometown for a second time means that I've finally stepped out of the shadow of my family—its history of alcoholism and dysfunction—and grown up.

I have friends who would tell me that this shows God has some kind of master plan and all of us are always "right where we should be." Well, tell that to someone who's just lost a child, or to a child whose parents have both been killed in a drive-by shooting, or to a father of four who's just lost his job because of the pandemic or to a woman just diagnosed with breast cancer, or...well, you get the picture.

No, I'm not talking about predestination or that we live in the best of all possible worlds. I'm describing what seems to me something even more miraculous: our God-given ability (I call it grace) not only to survive, but also to thrive, even when our best-laid plans fall through, and all appears out of control and hopeless.

This is what I think 12-steppers mean when they use GOD as an acronym for "Gift of Desperation." Time and time again, I've heard stories from people who, when their world seemed reduced to ugly rubble, found the strength to rebuild it in more beautiful ways than they'd ever thought possible.

And this is what gives me faith not only that my life will become fuller if I don't go cruising the coast of Norway, but also that we as a species, apparently lost in diseases, wars, and climate catastrophes none of us planned for, will learn to accept the grace to recognize that where we are is where we need to be to grow stronger, wiser, and more compassionate.

With Gratitude

God bless each of us as we travel on.
In our time of need
May we find a table spread in the wilderness
And companions on the road.
—Iona Abbey Worship Book

WHEN I FIRST BEGAN READING ABOUT PILGRIMS AND PILGRIMAGES, I imagined a solitary figure, staff in hand, striding over the landscape. And indeed, many authors who've written of their pilgrimage experiences seem to have wended their ways by themselves. I, however, have found that it's the companions on the road that have sustained me through my various journeys, many of whom you've met if you've read this book.

In the pilgrimage of writing and publishing these reflections, I have also been fed by many phenomenal people, beginning with my wife, Mary Lee, my first reader for every one of these tales from the journey. My sister, Jaye Sewall, has always been a companion (well, since I was five years old) and cheerleader. My Second Sundays Writing Group Leslie Bartlett, Lisa Fink, Charlie Priest, and Abbie Adam Ross—have given me all kinds of help. (If you think some of my sentences are long now, you should have read them before I submitted them to this group!) I thank Maureen Stanton,

With Gratitude

Barbara Walsh, Diane Benedict, and David Treadwell for reading the completed manuscript, and of course, the good folks of Maine Authors Publishing for making the manuscript a book.

Finally, I thank Michael Steinberg, mentor, taskmaster, and friend at the University of Southern Maine's Stonecoast MFA Program, from whom I learned most of what I know about writing nonfiction and who encouraged me to turn the "Geriatric Pilgrim" blogs into a book.

RIP, Mike.